NEL[illegible]

FOREWORD BY CHRIS ROLLINS

UNSHAKABLE

STANDING STRONG WHEN THINGS GO WRONG

REVISED AND EXPANDED

Published by Faith Journey Books U.S.A.

Printed in the United States of America

Library of Congress Cataloging-in-Publication Data
Searcy, Nelson
Unshakable : standing strong when things go wrong / Nelson Searcy
p. cm.
Includes bibliographical references.
ISBN 978-1-7363541-8-6 (pbk.)
1. Religion—Christian Life—Spiritual Growth

CONTENTS

For everyone who has ever struggled to stand strong through life's storms.

FOREWORD BY CHRIS ROLLINS

I like storms. I always have. It's not that I'm a "storm chaser," but growing up in beautiful Charleston, South Carolina, there is nothing like watching that dark grey charcoal wall looming large in the Atlantic Ocean and slowly moving into our city.

I've discovered that storms don't have to be chased — they come to you. In fact, if you are reading these words, you're either in a "storm" right now, you're headed into one, or you're coming out of one.

Storms are a fact of life.

One of my earliest storms that I remember is a broken family. I remember growing up in church, but that's not unusual in the Deep South. Like many families, we had religion, but not a personal relationship with Jesus. During my middle school years, our family had long since given up the charade and stopped going to church. My parents separated, headed for divorce. I was angry at my family. I was angry at God.

During the separation, my Dad died. That was the second major storm I remember facing. Maybe it was all a part of one major hurricane in my life. The separation was the landing, the front side of the storm. And just as I was getting used to my new circumstances (the quiet, calm, deceiving eye of the storm), the stronger, more destructive backside of the hurricane hit — my Dad's death.

To this day, I can remember literally crying out to God in my pain. Begging, I asked that if He were real that He would reveal Himself to me and rescue me. What I learned that day and have since discovered over and over again is that, "The Lord is close to the brokenhearted; he rescues those whose spirits are crushed." Psalm 34:18 (NLT)

A simple invitation would change my life. The youth group was going to camp the following week, and a friend invited me to go. It was in that youth group, through that youth pastor, and during that week of camp that I came to understand what a personal relationship with Jesus was truly all about. I gave my life to Christ and found a family, a Savior and a brand new purpose for life. It's hard to explain unless you've experienced it, but from the moment I gave my life to Christ, I felt the strong, unmistakable voice of God calling me to be a pastor.

The next storm I faced was of the actual hurricane variety. After high school, I went to Atlanta Christian College. It was there I met and married my wife, Janet. It was also there that I heard a second unmistakable call on my life — to plant a church back in my hometown of Charleston. This was long before it was "hip" to plant a church, long before church planting networks, and the resources available today. After graduation we moved to Charleston with no core group, no money and no job. But where God guides, He always provides. Janet quickly found a job teaching at an elementary school. I started meeting with people interested in helping us start a church.

But all of our plans and dreams would be dramatically halted.

Around midnight on September 22, 1989, Hurricane Hugo made landfall in Charleston. The landscape of the city and the lives of its people were forever changed. Charleston was devastated. However, God has a miraculous way of bringing something good out of something terrible. I now realize that Hurricane Hugo simply tilled the soil of people's hearts, preparing them and me for our new church.

Our first Sunday was Easter Sunday 1990. We met downtown in the Old Exchange Building, one of the most historic buildings in Charleston. My first sermon that Sunday was about what to do when you face a storm.

Over the next 14 years, every Sunday we set up and broke down all of our equipment. Honestly, we never really experienced any significant growth, even after purchasing a building. Lives were changed, people were loved, ministry occurred, but we were a small church — a church of about 125 people.

I recommitted my life to the Lord and to reaching lost people. I decided that I would not be the lid for the growth of our church. I became a voracious reader. I began reading everything I could get my hands on about leadership and systems. That's when I discovered Nelson Searcy. I joined one of his Coaching Networks and over the years worked my way up to his Advanced Coaching Network.

Best decision I ever made.

In the years that followed, our church experienced tremendous growth. We added another service and another. We built buildings. We hired staff. Eventually on Easter we had an all-time high attendance of over 3,000!

In 35 years, we've weathered a lot of storms, as I know you have as well. What I've learned is to work like it all depends on you, pray like it all depends on God, walk by faith, and trust Him with the results. He WILL see you through.

I am grateful to partner with Nelson to offer this practical book to help you grow in your faith and to stand strong when things go wrong. He has written this book to address some of the most common storms we all face in life — illness, financial stress, career challenges, family problems, doubt, lack of purpose, death, and more. So whether you're just coming out of a storm, you're heading into a storm, or you find yourself smack dab in the middle of one, my prayer is that this book will be a useful tool to help you stand strong — and be UNSHAKABLE!

Unshakable blessings,
Pastor Chris Rollins
Coastal Community Church
www.coastalcommunitychurch.org

HOW TO READ *UNSHAKABLE*

Did you read *Choose Your Own Adventure* books when you were growing up? You know, the series of children's books famous for letting the reader step into the role of the protagonist and decide how the story would unfold? I loved them. What could be better than a book you were actively involved in?

You could make choices for the main characters, steer the plot, read it how you wanted, even skip entire sections, and everything would still make sense. Now, that's reading! You can interact with this book in a similar way. Instead of simply reading *Unshakable* straight through, I invite you to *use* it. Read it however you'd like to. Let it fit your needs. After you move through the Introduction and the first two chapters on unshakable faith, choose the next chapter you read based on your current life circumstances.

Are you struggling financially? Turn to Chapter 11. Are you searching for purpose? Take a look at Chapter 3. Are you going through a difficult time with your family? Skip to Chapter 5. Are you facing a serious illness or caring for a loved one who is? Read Chapter 8. You get the picture. Each standalone chapter exists to help you face whatever storm is currently raging in your life with strength and ever-increasing faith.

Keep *Unshakable* close by in the weeks, months and years to come. Even if you aren't currently dealing with an issue the book addresses, you will eventually. Your life circumstances will shift, your needs will change and you will relate to each of the topics covered in new ways over time.

The Introduction: *Weathering the Storm*; Chapter 1: *The First Principle of Unshakable Faith;* and Chapter 2: *Six More Principles of Unshakable Faith* work together to launch every discussion. Make sure you read these chapters before moving on to more specific topics. As you interact with these pages, allow the truths and principles they contain to meet you where you are and point you toward peace, hope and unshakable faith.

INTRODUCTION

WEATHERING THE STORM

One summer, when I was 13, my family decided to take a trip to Myrtle Beach, South Carolina. I thought camping sounded much more fun than staying in a stuffy hotel, so my parents gave in to my pleas to rough it. They also agreed to let me bring along my best friend, Billy. As Mom and Dad loaded up our little camper with the week's necessities, Billy and I pulled together the supplies we would need to be able to survive the wild terrain of a South Carolina campground—music, chips, a couple of books, suntan lotion, soda, baseball gloves and two transistor radios . . . the essentials. We couldn't wait to get there and have some independence. If things went well, we were hoping we may even meet a few girls.

Little did we know that as we were making our way toward the beach, pulling the camper behind our old Chevy Impala and listening to Don Henley sing about the boys of summer, someone (or, I should say, some*thing*) else had the same destination in mind: a little storm named Hurricane Bob.

We were settled into our lot and just beginning to relax when we realized Bob was on his way—and moving fast. Now, this may not have been the most ferocious hurricane ever to hit the area, but that didn't matter. We weren't prepared to handle a hurricane of any size. Still, like many people do when they see a storm approaching, we decided we were going to try to ride it out. We battened down the hatches. We made sure everything was secured. We did all we knew to do and then climbed into the camper and waited for the storm to come.

At about 1:00 a.m., right on schedule, Bob came rolling through. Mom, Dad, Billy and I huddled together by the camper's one window and watched the wind whip broken tree limbs and loose lawn chairs through the air. I was terrified. I had never faced a storm like this in my life. The other campers had their lanterns on all around us, watching the damage unfold. Some were huddled by small camper windows like we were. Some were out in the elements, trying to hold down their tents and grills. We were all in this together.

As I watched the storm rage right before my eyes, I noticed something interesting: there were several brick houses on the edge of the campground that didn't look fazed at all. Most of the lights in the houses were off as if the people inside were sound asleep. Here I was, scared for my life, and 100 feet away, some other kid was probably in deep REM sleep, unaware of the havoc Bob was wreaking. I was instantly and thoroughly jealous of everyone in those brick houses.

Long story short, we made it through.

Over the next week, we had a great time camping, fishing, barbequing, body surfing in the ocean and, yep, meeting some girls. We bought T-shirts that read, "I survived Hurricane Bob." The storm we had ridden out together hadn't caused my parents, Billy or me any permanent damage. Still, I couldn't stop thinking about the difference between our experience of the storm, wide-eyed and trembling in our little camper, compared to the unfazed sleepers in those brick houses so close by—especially when I later learned that 18 people had died during Hurricane Bob's journey up the coast.

I wondered, *How could this hurricane be so devastating for some people and nothing more than a nuisance for others?* The answer didn't come to me right away, but over time I realized it is possible to survive a major hurricane unscathed if you have the right grounding.

As a pastor and a coach, I've had the opportunity to work with thousands of people facing hurt, fear, confusion and loss in various forms. No matter what those I talk with are going through—and no matter what I go through in my own life—when face-to-face with a difficult circumstance, I'm always reminded of the tenet originally born out of my run-in with Hurricane Bob so many years ago. It's a truth I turn to often and point others toward regardless of the circumstances raging in their world:

You can survive the storms of life if you have the right foundation.

Storms will come. They are inevitable, but you can be unshakable in their midst. You'll discover how in the pages ahead. Are you ready?

CHAPTER 1

THE FIRST PRINCIPLE OF UNSHAKABLE FAITH

A man of courage is also full of faith.

—Marcus Tullius Cicero

Anyone who listens to my teaching and follows it is wise, like a person who builds a house on solid rock. . . . But anyone who hears my teaching and doesn't obey it is foolish, like a person who builds a house on sand.

—Jesus (Matthew 7:24, 26)

A few years ago, my wife, Kelley, my son, Alexander, and I were staying at a friend's house. Late one night, after Kelley and Alexander had gone to bed, I decided to make use of my friend's office area to get some work done. As I was settling into the desk chair, I noticed a snake on the ground beside my foot. I froze. Then, doing my best not to disturb it, I slid out of the chair and retreated to the other side of the office. My heart was pounding. There are few things I despise more than snakes.

After some deep breaths to clear my head, I slipped out of the room and rummaged around in a couple of closets until I found a broom. The office had glass doors that opened to the yard (probably how the snake got in), so my plan was to stun the sucker with the handle of the broom, get those glass doors open and sweep it outside . . . all without getting bitten. I tiptoed back into the office. Sure enough, the snake was right where I had left him. I put my plan into action: Stun. Open. Sweep. It worked! Mission accomplished. The bad news was that I was too rattled to get any work done. When I finally calmed down, I headed to bed.

The next morning, I couldn't wait to tell Kelley how I had saved us from venom comas and certain death. As I poured her a cup of coffee, I said, "You're never going to believe this. There was a snake in the office last night and—"

"Was it a black snake?" she asked.

"Yeah, it was black. . . . I sat down right beside it, but it didn't move. So I eased out of the chair and snuck out of the office and found a broom—"

"Was it about this long?" She held her hands 16 inches or so apart.

"Yes . . ." I answered, wondering where these questions were coming from. "Anyway, I decided to stun it and then—"

Before I could finish my story, Kelley burst into laughter. I was a little offended by her response to my heroics.

"Why are you laughing?" I asked.

"I bought Alex that snake at the toy store yesterday!"

I have to admit, I was embarrassed. Here I was, thinking of myself as a snake wrangler on par with Indiana Jones, only to find that my nemesis had been a piece of plastic and rubber. But the whole scenario got me thinking . . .

Lots of times, we let things shake us that don't have to. Situations that seem overwhelming at first are often only child's play. We should be able to stay calm enough to step back and see things from the right perspective, but, by nature, we default to anxiety—even though God tells us not to be anxious about anything:

> *Don't worry about anything; instead, pray about everything. Tell God what you need, and thank him for all he has done.* (Philippians 4:6)

On the other hand, sometimes situations come into our lives that truly have the potential to shake us to our core. Uncertainty about our future, the death of a loved one, problems with our spouse, an unexpected illness or trouble with our kids are just a few examples of the many things that can throw us off course. As long as you and I are on this side of eternity, we will have to deal with difficulties. But here's a truth I want you to allow to sink into the depths of your being:

It is possible to survive the storms of life unscathed if you have the right foundation.

Before life's storms hit, bringing fear, uncertainty and even desperation, the first and most important thing you can do is ensure that you are building your life on a solid foundation.

PRINCIPLE I: SECURE A SOLID FOUNDATION

Whether you realize it or not, you are building your life on some foundation—a foundation that reflects whatever it is you have faith in. And you do have faith in something. We all do; we all have a set of beliefs through which we filter the world. Over time, those beliefs, whether positive or negative, build our foundation.

Take a minute to seriously consider the following questions: What do you have faith in? Who do you have faith in: yourself, your spouse, your business partners, a religious tradition, karma, the universe, an ephemeral God? What kind of faith foundation are you building your life on? When the wind starts whipping outside your window, how do you stay grounded?

Jesus once told a story about two different types of people—one who is constantly blown around by the storms of life and another who is always able to stand, no matter what the circumstances:

> *Anyone who listens to my teaching and follows it is wise, like a person who builds a house on solid rock. Though the rain comes in torrents and the floodwaters rise and the winds beat against that house, it won't collapse because it is built on bedrock. But anyone who hears my teaching and doesn't obey it is foolish, like a person who builds a house on sand. When the rains and floods come and the winds beat against that house, it will collapse with a mighty crash.* (Matthew 7:24–27)

When your faith is built on the right foundation, you can face life's problems—from the minor worries to the biggest tragedies—without being shaken. But if you put your faith in the wrong place, you will struggle when difficult circumstances come your way and, all too often, collapse completely when the intense storms of life start raging.

As I've mentioned, Hurricane Bob was my first lesson in the fact that having the right foundation is essential to being able to ride out a storm unscathed. But at that point in my life, I didn't know what the right foundation was. It wasn't until several years later that I discovered the truth that so many before me have known: the only foundation worthy of building on, and the only one strong enough to weather life's storms, is the foundation of faith in God and His Son, Jesus Christ. In the Gospels, Jesus Himself said:

> *I am the way, the truth, and the life. No one can come to the Father except through me.* (John 14:6)

Later, He asked His disciples—people who had walked with Him for years, seen Him perform miracles and listened to His teaching and His claims—this:

> *Who do you say I am?* (Mark 8:29)

Eventually, we all have to answer the same question: who do we believe Jesus is?

Who Is This Jesus?

There are only two possible answers. Either we fully embrace Jesus as who He says He is, or we reject His teachings totally and continue on our way. There is no middle ground. Take a look at how Cambridge University professor and former agnostic C. S. Lewis once positioned the options:

> I am trying here to prevent anyone saying the really foolish thing that people often say about Him: "I'm ready to accept Jesus as a great moral teacher, but I don't accept His claim to be God." That is the one thing we must not say. A man who was merely a man and said the sort of things Jesus said would not be a great moral teacher. He would either be a lunatic—on a level with the man who says he is a poached egg—or else He would be the Devil of Hell. You must make your choice. Either this man was, and is, the Son of God: or else a madman or something worse. You can shut Him up for a fool, you can spit at Him and kill Him as a demon; or you can fall at His feet and call Him Lord and God. But let us not come with any patronizing nonsense about His being a great moral teacher. He has not left that open to us. He did not intend to.[1]

When you and I acknowledge Jesus as the Son of God and accept the free gift of salvation that God has offered through Him (John 3:16), we gain forgiveness for our sins, a relationship with the One who created us and eternity in heaven. If you are ready to invite Jesus into your life, or if you'd like some more information for study, go to www.BeUnshakable.com. To read more about my personal story of faith, turn to the Epilogue.

With Jesus as your solid foundation, it is possible to remain unshakable no matter what kind of storms you face. Throughout the Scriptures, God has said He will give you unshakable faith as you trust Him with your life. In fact, He has committed to even more than that: He will give you peace, power, protection and a plan when things go wrong. Let's take a look at each of these four promises in detail.

Peace: God Will Give You Peace When You Are Anxious

Remember the Scripture I mentioned earlier in this chapter that says not to be anxious about anything? Those words were written by the apostle Paul, a man who faced intense persecution. He wrote the verses from a prison cell as a letter to the Christians in the city of Philippi. After instructing his readers not to worry, Paul went on to say that when we focus our attention on God, God will give us His peace:

> *Don't worry about anything; instead, pray about everything. Tell God what you need, and thank him for all he has done. Then you will experience God's peace, which exceeds anything we can understand. His peace will guard your hearts and minds as you live in Christ Jesus.* (Philippians 4:6–7)

Paul was simply expounding on Jesus' earlier words to a group of scared disciples:

> *Peace be with you.* (John 20:19)

As Paul described, those four words can wipe away your worries and anxieties and replace them with assurance—*if* you understand their power and lean into them.

The same God who created the galaxies, formed the heavens and the earth and knew you before you were born invites you to rest in His strength. His Son, Jesus, who raised the dead, caused blind men to see and overcame the grave, is the same one who says to us (and I paraphrase), "Hey, give your problems to Me." In Matthew, He (actually) says:

> *Come to me, all of you who are weary and carry heavy burdens, and I will give you rest.* (Matthew 11:28)

Given His resumé, I believe He can handle our burdens. But we must intentionally give them to Him. When we do, He promises to replace our anxiety with peace.

Power: God Will Give You Power When You Are Weak

Have you ever met someone who has it all together? Let me confirm something you may have suspected: that togetherness is 90% façade. None of us has everything together. People who act like they don't have a worry in the world usually hide the truth behind a carefully constructed exterior. They may impress us, but they don't impress God.

God is drawn to people willing to admit their weaknesses and rely on Him. He can give His power to those people, and they are usually more eager to accept it. The Bible is filled with examples of imperfect, ordinary, weak people whom God used to do extraordinary things.

When we try to match wits with life's storms in our power, we get beaten down pretty quickly. We can call on all of our resources and strength, but in the end, what we have isn't enough—something we can all attest to if we are honest with ourselves. Hiding our failure behind a forced smile and a façade of control doesn't improve anything. But when we are willing to admit our weaknesses and acknowledge God's strength, we start finding footing on the solid foundation He provides. As Paul wrote:

> *I can do everything through Christ, who gives me strength.* (Philippians 4:13)

Why would we even want to operate in our limited strength when we have access to God's unlimited power?

Protection: God Will Give You Protection When You Are Afraid

Fear is the most common of all human emotions. We are all afraid of something—sometimes with good reason, sometimes without. What are you afraid of? Is it something you're facing tomorrow? Something you're facing next year? Is it a financial problem? A health crisis? The loss of a relationship? Whatever you are afraid of, God is willing and able to stand as your protector in the face of that fear.

Our culture often perpetuates a misguided image of God. Too often, He is depicted as a feeble, white-haired old man who would seem to have little control over this spinning mass of earth. That image is completely wrong. Scripture paints the real picture:

> *The Lord is my rock, my fortress, and my savior; my God is my rock, in whom I find protection. He is my shield, the power that saves me, and my place of safety.* (Psalm 18:2)

These words were written by a great warrior named David. Every day, David faced the kind of fear and tragedy you and I can only imagine or maybe get a glimpse of through Hollywood epics. Still, he understood that God was his protector. In the same way that God protected David, He stands ready to protect you no matter what you face.

Plan: God Will Give You a Plan When You Are Uncertain

Uncertainty is a telling state of being. When the storms of life create uncertainty, you and I have a choice: we can either become insecure or look to God for direction. What we choose is a good indicator of the strength of our foundation. When we are not standing on solid rock, our natural tendency is to face uncertainty with an arrogance that stems from insecurity and breeds more insecurity. We pull inside ourselves and think, *I can handle this. I have the bank account/the education/the title/the intelligence (take your pick). I'll figure it out.* The irony is that facing uncertainty with this kind of perspective only brings greater uncertainty by piling more weight on a faulty foundation.

On the other hand, uncertainty can cause us to look to God. And since He is the only one who knows our future, He's the best one to look to:

> *"For I know the plans I have for you," says the* Lord. *"They are plans for good and not for disaster, to give you a future and a hope."* (Jeremiah 29:11)

God has the master plan for your life and mine. All we have to do is ask Him to lead us. Consider what James said about tapping into God's plan:

> *If you need wisdom, ask our generous God, and he will give it to you. He will not rebuke you for asking.* (James 1:5)

No matter what is causing uncertainty in your life, God has a plan for your peace and well-being on the other side. You can find your confidence by looking to Him.

THE RIGHT FOUNDATION

When you put your faith in Jesus as the foundation for your life—rather than putting it in family, friends, yourself, your work or anything else—God will give you His peace, His power, His protection and His plan. Only then will you be unshakable no matter what comes your way. When things go wrong, you won't be anxious. You'll allow yourself to rely on God's strength. You'll have the confidence and poise to move forward, knowing that He is protecting you. You will have peace about His plan for your future. From such a foundation of faith, you'll be able to sleep soundly through every dark night, no matter how fiercely the winds whip outside your window.

CHAPTER 2

SIX MORE PRINCIPLES OF UNSHAKABLE FAITH

A living faith will last in the midst of the blackest storm.

—Gandhi

I have told you all this so that you may have peace in me. Here on earth you will have many trials and sorrows. But take heart, because I have overcome the world.

—Jesus (John 16:33)

Building your life on a solid foundation of faith is the first and most important principle for standing strong when circumstances around you are spinning out of control. Just by stepping off of shifting sand and onto bedrock, you'll be more equipped to handle the challenges you face.

But there's more. Once you're on a solid foundation, there are six additional principles that can reinforce your ability to walk through every storm of life unscathed. Think of these six additional principles as pieces of a mosaic that, when taken together with the first, create a stunning image of strength and unshakable faith.

PRINCIPLE II: SIDESTEP SURPRISE

The situations that have the most potential to shake you are the ones that come out of nowhere: an unexpected diagnosis, a surprising layoff, an unforeseeable accident . . . When you're sideswiped by a problem you didn't see coming, it's easy to find yourself in a vulnerable position. Choosing not to be surprised by adverse circumstances is essential to standing strong in their midst.

You and I live in a fallen world full of difficult situations and disappointments. There's no getting around that fact. Jesus even told us we will face trouble throughout our lives, so why would we be surprised when it shows up? Take a look at what He said:

> *I have told you all this so that you may have peace in me. Here on earth you will have many trials and sorrows. But take heart, because I have overcome the world.* (John 16:33)

When we accept that problems and pain are unavoidable, we can sidestep the surprise that makes them even more difficult to deal with. God never promised that life on this side of heaven would be easy, even for those whose foundation is secured in Him. He simply promised to be with us every step of the way. We can take comfort in Jesus' assertion that He has already overcome every trial and tribulation we will face. We have the assurance of His peace.

PRINCIPLE III: ASK THE RIGHT QUESTION OF THE RIGHT PERSON RIGHT AWAY

When life goes wrong, your first instinct should be to turn to God. Too often, you and I look to every other possible source of comfort and insight. We ask our friends for advice, we buy self-help books, we turn inward and start mining our reserves. There's nothing inherently wrong with any of these things, but they shouldn't be our first stop. When we see signs of trouble brewing, our reflex should be to look to God. As James says:

> *Come close to God, and God will come close to you.* (James 4:8)

Not only do we need to turn to God immediately, but we also need to ask Him the right question. I'm sure you've known people in difficult situations who have spent their energy interrogating God rather than trusting Him. They ask, "Why me, God? Why me?" The real question is, "Why *not* me?" Why not you?

Again, none of us is immune to life's trials and tragedies. We live in a fallen world, and bad things will happen. Asking why doesn't accomplish anything. Next time you face a powerful storm that has the potential to shake you, try asking a different question. Ask *what* rather than *why*. Instead of giving into the common temptation of demanding, "Why did

You let this happen to me, God?" ask, "What do You want to teach me through this, God? What will You do in this situation to bring glory to Yourself?" Then listen for His answer.

PRINCIPLE IV: EMBRACE EMOTION

Once you have given God top priority in the storm you're facing, embrace the emotions you are feeling. Tune in to what's going on in your heart and mind. God gave you your emotions. He doesn't expect you to ignore or suppress them. Consider these words:

> *For everything there is a season, a time for every activity under heaven . . . . A time to cry and a time to laugh. A time to grieve and a time to dance.* (Ecclesiastes 3:1, 4)

You don't have to plaster on a smile and muscle through. It's okay to cry. It's okay to grieve. As you lean into God first, and then embrace the emotions your situation is stirring, He will use what you are feeling to draw you closer to Himself.

> *So then, since we have a great High Priest who has entered heaven, Jesus the Son of God, let us hold firmly to what we believe. This High Priest of ours understands our weaknesses, for he faced all of the same testings we do, yet he did not sin. So let us come boldly to the throne of our gracious God. There we will receive his mercy, and we will find grace to help us when we need it most.* (Hebrews 4:14–16)

PRINCIPLE V: BORROW FROM OTHERS

When you are feeling depleted, be quick to lean on the faith of the people around you for strength. To use a rudimentary analogy, think of your faith as a gas tank. Sometimes—especially amid a difficult situation—your gas tank runs low. But, at just the right moment, God brings other people around you who have full tanks. You can borrow from their reserves to make it to the other side.

The Bible emphasizes the importance of surrounding yourself with people you can borrow faith and strength from because you will never make it through life on yours alone. Even Moses, one of the great fathers of the faith, had to rely on the strength of others. As an old man, Moses was used by God to lead the Israelites to the Promised Land. He faced conflict and hardship at every turn. During one battle between the Israelites and a group of their enemies, Moses climbed a hill to oversee the fighting. As the battle progressed, God made an unusual appeal. God told Moses to raise his staff high above his head and said that, as long as he kept his staff raised, the Israelites would have victory. But if Moses dropped the staff, their enemies would be victorious.

Moses did the best he could to keep his staff lifted high, but eventually, his arms began to get tired. His back started to ache. His arthritis probably kicked in. Thankfully, he had people around him he could borrow strength from:

> *Moses' arms soon became so tired he could no longer hold them up. So Aaron and Hur found a stone for him to sit on. Then they stood on each side of Moses, holding up his hands. So his hands held steady until sunset. As a result, Joshua overwhelmed the army of Amalek in battle.* (Exodus 17:12–13)

There will come a time in your life when you won't be able to hold your arms up anymore. You won't be able to keep your chin up and continue pushing through. But if you surround yourself with a network of strong, faithful friends and family, they will be there to step in with the help you need.

Part of the reason God created the church was to give you and me a circle of like-minded people willing to come alongside us when we need support. Let me encourage you: if you aren't part of a local, biblically based church, find one. You need a community to worship, learn and serve with—people who will rejoice with you in good times and comfort you in difficult times, people who will lend you their faith and strength when you need it most.

When you share life with others who are building on the same foundation as you, your joys will be doubled and your burdens will be cut in half. For much more on the importance of being part of a strong church, I urge you to pick up my book *The New You: A Guide to Better Physical, Mental, Emotional, and Spiritual Wellness.* You will learn how the church is essential not only for your spiritual life but also for your overall health and well-being.

PRINCIPLE VI: BE A WILLING WITNESS

Your faithful journey through life's difficulties can be an incredible witness to other people if you allow it to be. Everyone you know is going to face failures, doubts, relationship problems, health issues and countless other difficulties that have the potential to shake them to their core. When you stand strong in the face of the same types of storms that wreak havoc in their lives, they will notice . . . and they will want to know how you do it. They will become curious about your faith. They will begin to consider their own foundation. When they ask where your strength comes from, be ready to answer:

> *In your hearts revere Christ as Lord. Always be prepared to give an answer to everyone who asks you to give the reason for the hope that you have. But do this with gentleness and respect.* (1 Peter 3:15 NIV)

Part of the good that will come out of the troubles you face will be your ability to relate to and help other people who are dealing with similar situations. Let yourself be a witness of God's faithfulness to those who turn to you.

PRINCIPLE VII: TURN PAIN INTO PURPOSE

In Romans 8:28, Paul wrote that God works all things together for the good of those who love Him: all things—even the layoffs, the rebellious kids, the breakups and the foreclosures. He is constantly weaving every circumstance you and I face into a beautiful tapestry. We tend to get hung up when we see a thread that's a color or texture we don't like, but when woven together with all of the other threads of our life, it enhances the overall masterpiece. Every pain serves a greater purpose. Every failure leads to a greater future if only we will let it.

A quick character study of people in the Bible who faced major difficulties and setbacks proves that God always worked things out for their good, just as He promises. For example, before Jesus was crucified, His disciple Peter—a man who had walked with Jesus throughout His earthly ministry—denied that he even knew Him. Major failure. Still, after Jesus' resurrection, God restored Peter, and he became the unshakable leader of the Christian church. To read more about Peter's story, turn to Chapter 4.

Mark struggled with storms of disconnection and fear as a teenager but rose to become a great leader and writer of Scripture. The apostle Thomas stood strong through the doubts that assailed him and went on to be an influential missionary. The Bible is filled with example after example of God turning the failures, flaws and pain of His people into substance for a greater purpose. He will do the same with yours.

WEATHERING THE STORM

Remember, unshakable faith has nothing to do with how strong you are and everything to do with how strong God is. No matter how smart, rich, connected or resourceful you consider yourself to be, you don't have what it takes to make it through life's toughest storms on your own. But as you build your life on the bedrock of God's strength and apply these timeless principles of unshakable faith to every difficult situation you face, you will be able to weather any storm that blows your way.

THE SEVEN PRINCIPLES OF UNSHAKABLE FAITH

Principle I:
Secure a Solid Foundation

Principle II:
Sidestep Surprise

Principle III:
Ask the Right Question of the Right Person Right Away

Principle IV:
Embrace Emotion

Principle V:
Borrow from Others

Principle VI:
Be a Willing Witness

Principle VII:
Turn Pain into Purpose

CHAPTER 3

LACK OF PURPOSE

Finding and Doing the Will of God

When your will is God's will, you will have your will.

—Charles H. Spurgeon

If you need wisdom, ask our generous God, and he will give it to you.

—James 1:5

Has your life gone off course? Do you wake up in the morning feeling like you should be doing something different with your time, something more? Are you considering giving up on a dream because it doesn't look like it's ever going to happen? Do you want to find your purpose and accomplish great things with your life, but you just aren't sure how to get started—or how to get started again?

Growing up, most of us have a clear mental image of how our future is going to unfold. We study and work toward that image, convinced we'll have everything we've ever dreamed of. But at some point along the way, many of us get off track.

Our plans don't play out the way we thought they would. Circumstances throw up roadblocks and detours.

Eventually, we realize that the vision we had for our lives isn't lining up with our current reality. We aren't where we wanted to be. This discrepancy between vision and actuality can make us feel frustrated and a little lost. Deep down, we know there's still something great in store for our lives—something more in line with what we've always envisioned—but we don't know exactly what it is or how to find it.

When we're in the middle of the storms of disappointment, unfulfilled potential and lack of direction, our minds inevitably turn to questions of purpose and significance. Even if we haven't considered God's will much in the past, we begin thinking about His potential plan for our lives and how it intersects with our daily to-do lists. And if we've always been cognizant that God has a will for our lives, we start wondering if we've missed it somehow.

Does God have a specific plan for your life and mine? Does He care if you're a doctor, a rock star or a stay-at-home parent? Does He care where you live and whom you marry?

Questions about the extent of God's involvement in our daily decisions have been debated for centuries. They're at the heart of the age-old discussion concerning the interplay between God's sovereignty and our free will. Many books have been written on the topic, so I won't go into the theological details here. Suffice it to say that God does care about the details of your life—and He wants to be involved in those details. For additional resources and deeper study on the theology of God's will, go to www.BeUnshakable.com.

God wants nothing more than for you to know His purpose for you and to align yourself with it. When you do, He can bless you abundantly and direct you into the life He has in store. Consider what the psalmist wrote:

> *The Lord says, "I will guide you along the best pathway for your life.*
> *I will advise you and watch over you."* (Psalm 32:8)

Given that promise, how is it that so many of us feel like we are living a subpar life full of drudgery and dissatisfaction? When you and I find ourselves drifting, separated from God's will, it's for one of two reasons: either we have intentionally chosen to ignore God's calling and go our own way, or we simply don't know how to discern what His will is for our lives.

If you are struggling with a lack of direction and purpose, you can rest assured that God has more in store for you than the life you are currently living. He wants to guide you along the best pathway. He wants you to know His will. What is His will exactly? God's will is the highest and best plan for your life. It is the direction you would choose if you could see things from His perspective.

God's will is the highest and best plan for your life. It is the direction you would choose if you could see things from His perspective.

God created you and knows you better than you know yourself. In your understanding, you operate with limited information, but God already knows how your story plays out in its entirety. He has the master plan, and He wants to lead you down the best path to all that is in store for you.

So you have a choice to make. You can either continue to stumble through each day, filled with the stress and uncertainty that come with operating in your own power, or you can choose to invite God into your plans and surrender your life to His will. Submitting to God's will doesn't mean things will always be perfect. There are still going to be valleys, but they aren't going to be as low. And the peaks will be even higher. When you allow God to begin directing your steps, you will finally find your sweet spot and experience the satisfaction of living the life you were created to live.

DISCOVERING AND DOING GOD'S WILL

You and I face crossroads every day. These crossroads are the big and small decisions that shape our lives. Each one is an opportunity to seek God, move forward in step with Him and get closer to the center of His will. My wife, Kelley, and I found ourselves at a major crossroads several years ago. When Kelley and I got married, we knew we would probably never have children. Kelley had dealt with some health issues early in her life that made a future pregnancy unlikely. So for the first ten years of our marriage, we rolled along as a happy DINK (double income no kids) couple.

Shortly after making a cross-country move from Southern California to New York City to start The Journey Church, we heard about an experimental fertility treatment being conducted at Columbia University. Given the details of our situation, we were perfect candidates. But even though the thought of having a baby was exciting, we didn't want to move ahead without making sure this treatment was in God's plan for us. We decided to spend some time intentionally focusing our attention on the first of three important steps for finding and doing God's will—actively listening to God.

Step One: Actively Listen to God

You and I are wired to crave certainty, so we tend to think of God's will in terms of a roadmap. We want to know what our destination is, how many turns it will take to get there and what detours we'll run into. But God's will isn't a map detailing the way from point A to point B; it's a lifestyle of fellowship with the cartographer. And because it's a lifestyle, our guidance comes daily rather than all at once. That's why following God's purposes requires faith; we can't always see the destination, but we know God will direct us the right way if we pay attention to His voice every day of the journey:

> *Serve only the LORD your God and fear him alone. Obey his commands, listen to his voice, and cling to him.* (Deuteronomy 13:4)

When you don't know which way to turn in your career, in a relationship or in any other big decision you need to make, actively listening to God is essential. You can't follow His guidance if you can't hear what He's saying. You may be thinking, *I would love to hear from God, but He's not talking.* Here's some good news: God isn't being silent in your situation; He is always speaking to you. You just have to learn to hear Him.

Have you ever been in the middle of a phone conversation with someone when the connection got weak and crackly, or the call dropped altogether? One of you moved out of range, and the signal was lost. When you are close to God and actively listening for His voice, you can hear what He is saying. But when you step out of range, the conversation ends—not because He isn't speaking anymore, but because you've lost connection. Sometimes we move out of the range of His voice without meaning to. Other times, we step away on purpose because we want to do our own thing. Either way, the Scriptures warn that there are dangers to not listening to what God has to say:

> *If you refuse to listen to the LORD your God and to obey the commands and decrees he has given you, all these curses will pursue and overtake you until you are destroyed.* (Deuteronomy 28:45)

None of us wants to be swept away by curses or face destruction, to put it mildly. And we're eager to listen to God because we know He guides us toward our true purpose. So how can we better connect? The key lies in recognizing the ways He communicates with us.

God speaks in two primary ways. The first is *direct revelation.* Through the direct revelation of the Bible, God has already given us His input and wisdom on thousands of issues we wrestle with. He has clarified many specifics about His will in His inspired Word, but we continue to struggle and stress because we don't spend time seeking out what He says. If we just open the Scriptures and look, we can find the answers to a lot of our questions.

God also speaks through *daily guidance.* As we've established, He doesn't reveal His will for us all at once. Following God's purposes is a little like driving a car at night: you can only see a few feet in front of you, but you can make the whole trip that way. When Moses led the Israelites into the desert on their way to the Promised Land, God taught them to trust Him by providing just enough food for each day (Exodus 16). Whatever wasn't eaten perished overnight, so they had to trust Him to provide anew each morning. In the same way, you and I have to trust God to give us daily guidance for our lives.

Two Ways God Speaks:

Direct Revelation
Daily Guidance

God's daily communication comes in several ways:

- First, for those of us who are Christians, the Holy Spirit is inside of us, prompting us and guiding us in the direction of God's will. Sometimes we feel the Holy Spirit as an inkling in our conscience, or we'll hear the still, small voice in our heart calling out to us.

- Second, God gives us daily guidance through prayer. Spending time in prayer every day is key to growing our relationship with God and hearing His voice. We have to be careful not to fall into the trap of doing all of the talking in our prayer time; we must make sure we are listening too.

- Third, God guides us through the counsel of other mature Christians.
- Fourth, God will orchestrate the circumstances in our lives to direct us in a certain way—something we often recognize better in hindsight.

When Kelley and I were faced with the opportunity to pursue fertility treatment, we wanted to make sure we heard from God before we moved ahead with anything. Our first step was to go to God's Word. We asked ourselves, *Does the Bible have anything to say that could inform this decision? Is there anything about pursuing fertility treatment that would be against His will?* In Genesis 2, God says, "Be fruitful and multiply." So we took that as a positive.

We spent a lot of time in prayer, seeking God's direction on the potential of creating a family in this way. Then we sought counsel from some friends who had gone through various types of fertility treatment. They gave us first-hand insight into the emotional pitfalls we could run into but also what joy could come if the treatment worked. While we were wrestling with all of this, several circumstances in our lives seemed to start lining up in a way that would be conducive to the treatment. We felt comfortable that God was behind the plan, so we decided to go for it.

You don't have to make the important decisions in your life on your own—or the seemingly small decisions, for that matter. God is ready and willing to direct you into the abundant life He promises. He is constantly speaking to you and pointing you toward His purpose for your life. The question is whether or not you are listening. As Jesus said:

> *Anyone with ears to hear should listen and understand.* (Luke 8:8)

The number one reason you and I don't hear from God is because we don't want to. We are afraid that we won't like what He says and that we won't want to obey. So we claim He isn't speaking. That way, we can continue doing what seems right to us, what is comfortable, even if it's not beneficial. But when we fully grasp the reality that no matter how God directs us, His plan is better than anything we could ever come up with on our own, then we will be eager to hear from Him and respond accordingly:

> *Now to Him who is able to do exceedingly abundantly above all that we ask or think, according to the power that works in us.* (Ephesians 3:20 NKJV)

When we trust God and lean into His will, He is able to do exceedingly abundantly above all that we can ask or think, according to the power of Jesus Christ. Nowhere in that promise will we find a lack of fulfillment, drudgery, tension or anxiety. God offers us more than we can imagine if we only listen to Him and obey Him quickly—which is the second step in discovering and doing His will.

Step Two: Act Quickly on What God Says

My and Kelley's decision to move ahead with the fertility treatment kicked off a four-month process of tweaking her medications and undergoing test after test. When the morning of the first treatment finally arrived, we showed up at the doctor's office early and excited. The first thing they did was draw Kelley's blood. A couple of hours later, as we were prepping for liftoff, the doctor walked in and said, "We won't be able to do the first treatment today—because you are pregnant!" We were shocked. Turns out, the process of changing Kelley's medication leading up to the first treatment had balanced the hormone levels in her body, and we were able to conceive naturally. Nine months later, we had our son, Alexander.

Listening to God and then acting when He told us to move forward resulted in our being able to conceive a child in a way that previously seemed impossible. If we had been slow to act when we heard God saying to go ahead, nothing would have changed in our situation. God used the Columbia experiment to put us on a path. We had no idea we wouldn't have to go through with the actual treatments, but God did. All He asked of us was to listen to His direction and then act quickly on what He said to do. We are glad we did—and so is Alexander!

I have noticed a trend while counseling hundreds of people trying to find God's will. Those who feel frustrated with God and His plan are often holding something back from Him. They say they want to figure out God's purpose for their lives, but they don't really want to hear from Him because they're afraid they'll disagree.

For example, I've met Christians who won't pray about a current relationship because they know God's answer would be to end it. Or they are hesitant to seek God's will for their career because they might be pushed out of their comfort zone. Their attitude reflects what one well-known singer/songwriter sang: "I'll do whatever you want, God, just let me have my way." They give lip service to God's sovereignty, but when it comes right down to it, they want to be in charge.

Delayed obedience is disobedience.

God is more than willing to show you His incomparable will, but you get to choose if you obey and when. The longer you delay obedience, the more you suffer. Why? Because delayed obedience is disobedience. When you do obey, on the other hand, it's like putting a key in the right lock and opening a door. You will be surprised by how much guidance will be suddenly available to you. You will have access to the abundant life God promises. Many times, God is waiting for you to say yes to Him before He will show you the next step.

> *But don't just listen to God's word. You must do what it says. Otherwise, you are only fooling yourselves.* (James 1:22)

If you aren't willing to act quickly when you hear God speaking, you will remain stuck in a rut of unfulfillment, confusion and lack of direction. When God tells you to do something, don't delay. There's danger in disobedience:

> *Be careful that you do not refuse to listen to the One who is speaking. For if the people of Israel did not escape when they refused to listen to Moses, the earthly messenger, we will certainly*

> *not escape if we reject the One who speaks to us from heaven!* (Hebrews 12:25)

Is there something you know you should be doing in your life right now—something God has told you to do—that you haven't done? Take that step. When you say yes to God, He will show you the next phase of His will for your life. He will lead you along the path to blessing:

> *Now that you know these things, God will bless you for doing them.* (John 13:17)

Step Three: Admit Complete Dependence on God

The third step in finding and doing God's will is admitting your complete dependence on Him. Our culture values independence, but if you think about it, independence is easy. There's nothing to it. Any rebellious person can go his own way and ride off into the sunset in search of whatever he wants. Strength is found in humility—in understanding the power of submitting selfish desires to the Creator's bigger perspective.

The path to doing God's will and experiencing His blessing is found at the end of our self-sufficiency. That's where we recognize that He has the best plan for our lives. Everyone comes to a point where they have to decide if they are going to plow ahead with their wants and desires or submit themselves to God's more significant, better purposes. As C. S. Lewis wrote:

> There are only two kinds of people in the end: those who say to God, "Thy will be done," and those to whom God says, in the end, "Thy will be done."[2]

Over 2,000 years ago, about 48 hours before His crucifixion, Jesus faced this moment of decision. Alone in the garden of Gethsemane, He had a choice to make. He could ignore the path God had for Him, flee Jerusalem and live the rest of His life doing His own thing, or He could align Himself with God's greater plan. Here's how Matthew described the scene:

> *[Jesus] went on a little farther and bowed with his face to the ground, praying, "My Father! If it is possible, let this cup of suffering be taken away from me. Yet I want your will to be done, not mine."* (Matthew 26:39)

Jesus took the position of strength by putting God's plan for His life over His own desire. He submitted to God's authority, saying, "Your will, not mine." He knew God's plan was the highest and that, ultimately, it would produce the greatest good and glory—not only for Him but also for the entire human race.

Unshakable Principle I:

Secure a Solid Foundation

Thanks to Jesus' sacrifice, you and I can be reconciled to God and participate in the abundant life He offers as we earnestly seek and obey Him. Think back to Principle I of Unshakable Faith: *Secure a Solid Foundation.* When you trust God with your life and say yes to building your future on the foundation of His Son, God will give you *His* peace, *His* power, *His* protection and *His* plan—four things essential to living out your purpose.

Until you say yes to God's offer of salvation, you will continue to be barraged by the storms of confusion and unfulfillment. You won't be able to engage with His incredible story for your life. Be willing to submit to Him in every area. That means admitting your dependence on Him for your day-to-day life and eternity.

DISCOVERING GOD'S BEST

In the face of the experimental fertility treatment Kelley and I were offered, we were committed to finding and doing God's will. We didn't want to take a single step toward the treatment if it wasn't part of God's best plan for us. That's why we spent a lot of time actively listening for His direction. When we knew what He was telling us, we were quick to move. And all along, we were aware of our complete dependence on God. If we had gone through the entire treatment process and still wound up unable to have kids, we would have been okay; we would have walked away knowing we had followed God's plan and that His purposes were being worked out.

To find and do God's will, you and I must follow this pattern in every area of our lives—not just at major crossroads but in our daily decisions and interactions. God isn't hiding His will from us. He wants us to know what it is so we can step into the best that He has for us. We may not always get God's direction precisely right, but He will honor our efforts to honor Him.

Consider the words of writer Thomas Merton in his work *Thoughts in Solitude*:

> My Lord God, I have no idea where I am going. I do not see the road ahead of me. I cannot know for certain where it will end. Nor do I really know myself, and the fact that I think I am following your will does not mean that I am actually doing so. But I believe that the desire to please you does in fact please you. And I hope I have that desire in all that I am doing. I hope that I will never do anything apart from that desire. And I know that if I do this you will lead me by the right road, though I may know nothing about it. Therefore I will trust you always though I may seem to be lost and in the shadow of death. I will not fear, for you are ever with me, and you will never leave me to face my perils alone.[3]

The desire to please God pleases God. Our responsibility is to demonstrate that desire by eagerly seeking Him, wholly obeying Him and fully acknowledging that He is our ultimate source, supply and guide. When we are willing to do these three things, we will wake up every morning on the path of peace and purpose. Never again will we have to be blown around by the storms of confusion and lack of direction because we will be continually moving right into the center of God's perfect will.

CHAPTER 4

FAILURE

Embracing the True Nature of Failure

Failure is, in a sense, the highway to success, inasmuch as every discovery of what is false leads us to seek earnestly after what is true.

—John Keats

And we know that God causes everything to work together for the good of those who love God and are called according to his purpose for them.

—Paul (Romans 8:28)

The word *failure* is full of negative connotations. It's connected with so many other words we don't like—*disappointment, inadequacy* and *inferiority*, to name a few. But what if I told you that, when it comes to failure, we've all been sold a bill of goods? What if I told you that failure is actually a positive thing when viewed from the proper perspective? That it is a necessary element to all of our achievements? Would you believe me?

The truth is that failure is the primary building block of every success you've ever had. Just think back over your life. When you were learning to walk, you fell countless times.

Each time you got back up, you were a little sturdier. The first time you played baseball, you whiffed every ball that came toward you, but with practice, you began making contact. When you were learning to drive, you didn't whip right into your first parallel parking space, did you? You had to back up and try it again . . . and again.

Life is a process of growing through a series of failures that shape your ability to succeed. The key is to have the right perspective on failure. If you see failure as a dead end, it will destroy you. If you see it as a stepping stone to greater things, that's precisely what it will be. As the famed American soccer player Kyle Rote Jr. once said, "There is no doubt in my mind that there are many ways to be a winner, but there is really only one way to be a loser, and that is to fail and not look beyond the failure."[4]

Life is a process of growing through a series of failures that shape your ability to succeed.

When the storms of failure start raging in your life, you have a choice: you can either use failure as an excuse to give up or let your failure grow you up. If you choose to use failure as a catalyst for your growth, every failure you face will be an opportunity to move closer to the life God has in store for you.

HISTORICAL FAILURES

History is full of success-through-failure stories. While living, Vincent Van Gogh was a failure as an artist. He only sold one painting in his lifetime, and that was just four months before his death. But despite his failure, he kept pressing on; he kept pursuing his art, and now he is one of history's most respected artists. Today, his paintings sell for over $100 million each. Good thing he didn't choose to quit when failure loomed around every corner.

Michael Jordan, one of the greatest basketball players ever, was cut from his high school team. Failure. During his professional career, he missed over 12,000 shots, lost over 400 matchups and flubbed over 25 last-minute baskets that would have won the game. Yet Jordan became an NBA Hall of Famer and a living legend because he understood that failures are the bones on which successes are fleshed out.

Or take the story of the man who, at age 22, lost his job; at 23, was defeated in his run for state legislature; at 24, failed in a new business venture; at 26, dealt with the death of his longtime sweetheart; at 27, had a nervous breakdown; at 29 and 34, was defeated again and again for political office; at 45, lost his run for the US Senate; at 47, was defeated in his nomination for vice president; at 49, was once again defeated in his run for the Senate; but at 51, became the president of the United States. This failure was named Abraham Lincoln, one of the greatest presidents to ever live.

Abraham Lincoln faced more failures before his 40th birthday than many of us will face in a lifetime, but he refused to give up and wallow in self-pity. Instead, he allowed his failures to cultivate a strong character within—a character that was necessary for the tasks he was later called to. Many historians believe Lincoln could do what needed to be done in the Civil War because of the faith and perseverance he had developed over many years of dealing with failure. Because Lincoln viewed his failures in the right light, they paved the way for his respected place in history.

FAILING FORWARD

When you and I deal with failure well, God uses the experience to prepare us for the next thing He has in store. Consider the life of Jesus' disciple Peter. When Jesus started His earthly ministry and called Peter to follow Him, Peter was busy running his family's fishing business. Still, this quick-tempered fisherman understood that there was something special about Jesus, so he left his fishing nets behind and set out with the rest of the disciples. Peter quickly became one of Jesus' inner circle. A few years later, Jesus went so far as to call Peter the rock on which He would build His church (Matthew 16:18).

One night close to the time of the crucifixion, Jesus and His disciples were having dinner together. As they talked about the kingdom of God and things to come, Jesus made a prediction. He said that one of those closest to Him—in fact, one of the people sitting around the dinner table—would betray Him. We know in hindsight that the betrayer was Judas, but the other disciples started worrying if it would be them. So later that evening when Jesus told his disciples that all of them would desert Him, Peter felt the need to prove that it wouldn't be him. He stood up and said (and I paraphrase), "Not me, Lord. It's not going to be me. I am loyal. I will never betray You." And Jesus said to Peter (again paraphrasing), "Peter, don't be so sure. There will come a time when, in my hour of greatest need, you will deny me three times in the same night" (Matthew 26).

Fast-forward to later that night. The Jewish officials arrested Jesus. All of His disciples were terrified. The arrest didn't fit with their understanding of Jesus as the Messiah and His plan for God's kingdom. And since Jesus was their leader, they reasoned that they were probably next on the religious leaders' hit list. So they scattered—all but Peter. He stayed close to where Jesus was being held to see what was happening.

In Matthew's account of that night, he wrote that while Peter was sitting outside in the courtyard, a servant girl came over and said, "I recognize you! You were one of those guys with Jesus." Peter said, "Not me!" (Matthew 26, paraphrased). Denial number one.

Peter went on to deny knowing Jesus two more times that night. As the third denial left his lips, he heard a rooster's crow signal the dawn, and he remembered Jesus' prophecy. Peter had failed. After years of trusting Jesus as Lord, he had renounced him three times on the same night. Feeling like a complete failure, Peter ran back to his family's fishing business.

Some days later, after Jesus' crucifixion and resurrection, Peter had an encounter with Jesus that cast a new light on his failure:

> *Later, Jesus appeared again to the disciples beside the Sea of Galilee. This is how it happened. Several of the disciples were there—Simon Peter, Thomas (nicknamed the Twin), Nathanael from Cana in Galilee, the sons of Zebedee, and two other disciples.*

Simon Peter said, "I'm going fishing."

"We'll come, too," they all said. So they went out in the boat, but they caught nothing all night.

At dawn, Jesus was standing on the beach, but the disciples couldn't see who he was. He called out, "Fellows, have you caught any fish?"

"No," they replied.

Then he said, "Throw out your net on the right-hand side of the boat, and you'll get some!" So they did, and they couldn't haul in the net because there were so many fish in it.

Then the disciple Jesus loved said to Peter, "It's the Lord!" When Simon Peter heard that it was the Lord, he put on his tunic (for he had stripped for work), jumped into the water, and headed to shore. The others stayed with the boat and pulled the loaded net to the shore, for they were only about a hundred yards from shore. When they got there, they found breakfast waiting for them—fish cooking over a charcoal fire, and some bread.

"Bring some of the fish you've just caught," Jesus said. So Simon Peter went aboard and dragged the net to the shore. There were 153 large fish, and yet the net hadn't torn.

"Now come and have some breakfast!" Jesus said. None of the disciples dared to ask him, "Who are you?" They knew it was the Lord. Then Jesus served them the bread and the fish. This was the third time Jesus had appeared to his disciples since he had been raised from the dead.

After breakfast Jesus asked Simon Peter, "Simon son of John, do you love me more than these?"

"Yes, Lord," Peter replied, "you know I love you."

> *"Then feed my lambs," Jesus told him.*
>
> *Jesus repeated the question: "Simon son of John, do you love me?"*
>
> *"Yes, Lord," Peter said, "you know I love you."*
>
> *"Then take care of my sheep," Jesus said.*
>
> *A third time he asked him, "Simon son of John, do you love me?"*
>
> *Peter was hurt that Jesus asked the question a third time. He said, "Lord, you know everything. You know that I love you."*
>
> *Jesus said, "Then feed my sheep."*
>
> *"I tell you the truth, when you were young, you were able to do as you liked; you dressed yourself and went wherever you wanted to go. But when you are old, you will stretch out your hands, and others will dress you and take you where you don't want to go." Jesus said this to let him know by what kind of death he would glorify God. Then Jesus told him, "Follow me."* (John 21:1–19)

Peter had denied Jesus three times, so Jesus restored him by asking him to pledge his devotion three times. Then, in the same way as He first called Peter to be His disciple, Jesus again said to him, "Follow me." Peter did. He went on to become one of the greatest leaders of the early church. He served as the pastor of Jerusalem's church and started a missionary movement that turned the known world upside down over the next forty years. Peter found his greatest success in life after his greatest failure because he did not let his failure keep him from being used by God.

Peter's story provides an excellent example of the four keys to walking through failure with unshakable faith. First, face the emotions associated with your failure. Second, allow your failure to draw you closer to God. Third, identify and learn from the source of your failure. Finally, find and obey God's new plan for your life. When you approach every failure you face with these four things in mind, your failures will genuinely become the building blocks for your ultimate success. Let's look at each in more detail.

Face the Emotions Associated with Your Failure

None of us likes to come up short. Peter failed Jesus three times, and, just as we would, he had an intense emotional reaction to his failures. After the third denial, Peter was so upset that he threw his hands up and went back to his old way of life.

You can probably relate on some level. I know I can. When you and I fail at something—whether it's at a job, a relationship or a personal goal we've set for ourselves—we face a barrage of emotions that make us want to give up altogether. The more closely we identify with the area of our failure, the harder it is to keep moving forward. That's why, in general, men have a more difficult time dealing with career failures, while women are more devastated by relational failures. Failure affects each of us differently, depending on the circumstances, our life experiences and our makeup.

Don't be surprised by the intense emotions that come along with facing a setback. More importantly, please don't ignore them. Remember Principle IV of Unshakable Faith: *Embrace*

Emotion. Acknowledge the feelings of fear, anger, blame or shame barraging you and work through them. Get to the other side so you can focus on the future. As the apostle Paul wrote,

Unshakable Principle IV: Embrace Emotion

> *No, dear brothers and sisters, I have not achieved it* [in other words, I have failed], *but I focus on this one thing: Forgetting the past and looking forward to what lies ahead.* (Philippians 3:13)

When the storms of failure are raging, these two essential steps will help you embrace the emotions you are feeling and move past them:

1. Surround yourself with strong, godly people who will encourage you and refuse to let you fall into despair.

2. Talk to Jesus about your failure. Be brutally honest about how you feel. Admit your disappointment and frustration to Him. He will help you get back up and heading in the right direction. Remember Hebrews 4:14–16.

Allow Your Failure to Draw You Closer to God

Failure doesn't separate you from God. He is not disappointed in you, and He's not pointing an "I told you so" finger in your direction. Just the opposite: God wants to use your failure to draw you closer to Himself.

In the midst of difficulty, most people have one of two initial reactions to God—they either pull away from Him in shame and anger or allow their disappointment to draw them closer to Him. Going back to Peter's story, notice how he initially let his failure push him away from God. He returned to being a fisherman and threw out the whole idea of God having a bigger plan for his life. But, to use Peter's failure for good, Jesus sought Peter out. That led to a turning point. When Peter recognized that Jesus wasn't disappointed in him, he ran (well, swam) back to the relationship and was restored. God wants to use everything you go through in life to draw you closer to Him, but the choice is ultimately yours to make.

> ***If you are letting your failure push you away from God, you are making the wrong choice.***

Is there a failure in your life that is preventing you from drawing closer to God? Is there a relationship that has ended, a marriage that is on the rocks or a career that's not going the way you wanted it to? Do you struggle with a reoccurring sin that you can't seem to conquer and that makes you feel like you don't deserve God's love? If you are letting your failure push you away from God, you are making the wrong choice. Follow Peter's later example: jump out of the boat and get to God as fast as you can.

Identify and Learn from the Source of Your Failure

If you don't learn from your failure, you waste it. So one of your first steps when you fail should be to identify the root of the problem. For example, pride was one of the major reasons for Peter's failure. When Jesus told the disciples that they would all desert Him, Peter arrogantly assured Jesus that he would never do that. And yet we all know the rest of the story. Peter's arrogance led to his downfall, but in due course, he learned humility.

Once you figure out what caused your failure, glean whatever insight you can from that knowledge. Every failure is an integral part of your growth. Think of failure as a test. When you identify the cause of it and learn from it, you pass the test. By passing, you become stronger, wiser and more prepared to step into God's plan for your future. Never forget that God is continually working everything together for the good of those who love Him (Romans 8:28).

Find and Obey God's New Plan for Your Life

Esteemed businessman and author Zig Ziglar said, "Failure is a detour, not a dead-end street." When you give your failure over to God, He will exchange it for a new plan. He will replace your negative emotions with strength and faith. When God is involved, failure is never final:

> *The godly may trip seven times, but they will get up again. But one disaster is enough to overthrow the wicked*
> (Proverbs 24:16)

Get back up, hand your disappointment to God and listen for His new plan for your life. Failure should never prevent you from reaching your God-given potential; it should be a building block to help you get there. To read more about how to discern God's will for your life, turn to Chapter 3.

Here's how Peter's story ended: as Christianity spread into the Roman Empire, the area became more and more hostile toward Christians. The Roman Emperor Nero burned Christians at the stake for their faith. Thousands were crucified. Ultimately, Peter was arrested for being a Christian leader. Upon his arrest, the Roman officials told Peter that if he would deny Jesus as Lord and claim the authority of Caesar, they would let him live. If he refused, he would be crucified. Think about the irony. Peter, whose ultimate failure was denying Christ, now had his life on the line. One more quick denial, and he would be free to live the rest of his natural life any way he wanted. But he refused. As a result, he was sentenced to death on a cross. When the time came for Peter to be crucified, he protested that he was not worthy to die in the same manner as his Lord and asked to be crucified upside down. Peter went from fisherman to follower to failure . . . to martyr.

When you embrace the positive implications failure can have and commit to seeking after God in your pain and disappointment, He will give you the unshakable faith and strength to face whatever the future holds. One day, your story of perseverance may be the story that inspires others to press through and build on failure in search of their own ultimate success.

CHAPTER 5

FAMILY PROBLEMS

Dealing with the Dysfunction

A family in harmony will prosper in everything.

—Chinese Proverb

But as for me and my family, we will serve the Lord.

—Joshua 24:15

One evening, Kelley and I stopped into a small boutique in our neighborhood after dinner. While browsing, I came across a decorative plaque that read, "Remember, as far as anyone knows, we are a nice, normal family." The shopkeeper noticed my chuckle and said the plaque had been a huge seller. It resonated with people. Well, my interest was piqued. I went home and did some research on the licensing of the quotation. As it turns out, marketers have slapped these words on everything from clocks to coasters. Sales have skyrocketed in the last couple of years.

Why do so many people relate to the sentiment? Because, deep down, we all feel like our families aren't quite what they should be. There are skeletons in our closets. There are old scars and new wounds left by broken marriages, wayward children and countless disappointments, both big and small. Even though we don't like the word, most of us worry at one point or another that our families may border on being (gasp) dysfunctional. So we do our best to portray a nice, normal image around our friends and acquaintances, so much so that marketers are making a fortune from the dichotomy.

Here's some comforting news: every family is dysfunctional. The question is, to what degree? Family can be a source of great comfort and grounding, but it can also be a hotbed for conflict, unresolved tension and grudges that have the potential to whip up significant storms. Thankfully, there are steps we can take to keep our families strong and ensure they are consistently safe havens of love and support. We don't have to struggle through family strife with plastered-on smiles; that's not what God intends. Instead, He wants us to cultivate unshakable families that can stand firmly together amid any storm blowing through.

FIRST EQUALS BLESSING

Creating the family was God's first priority after He set the world in motion. As Genesis describes, God made Adam and Eve and then told them to get busy having kids or, as He put it, "be fruitful and multiply" (Genesis 1:26–28). With that, the first family was established. But even though the family is an institution created and ordained by God, He never promises that family life will be perfect. He does, however, tell us that we can have strong, flourishing families if we decide to put Him at the head.

One of the most powerful principles in Scripture is what I like to refer to as *The Principle of the First.* The Principle of the First holds that God will bless the areas of your life where you put Him first. First equals blessing. If you want God to bless your finances, you have to put Him first in your finances. If you want Him to bless your friendships, put Him first in your friendships. The same goes for family.

Putting God first in your family means actively trusting Him as the foundation for your family's life and relinquishing your desire for control. There are three practical steps you can take to put God first:

1. Intentionally focus your family on God every day.
2. Be quick to forgive your family members when they wrong you.
3. Prioritize quality time with your family.

Let's explore each one of these in detail.

Focus Your Family on God

Building a family is similar to building a house. Every good builder knows that the most important element of building a strong house is to lay a solid foundation. That way, the structure will be secure and able to stand against the elements. Think back to Principle I of Unshakable Faith: *Secure a Solid Foundation.* On an individual level, this means trusting God with your life by accepting salvation through Jesus. On a family level, securing a solid foundation means focusing your family on God daily through prayer and Bible study.

You can't control anyone's heart but your own. You can't force your spouse, children, siblings or extended family into a relationship with Jesus. But you can establish your family on the solid foundation of spending time with God by being intentional about praying and studying His Word together. Not only will that create a secure base for your family life, but it will also lay essential groundwork for the members of your family who don't know Jesus to come to the point of accepting His love. Those who do know Him will grow into deeper relationship and live out His truth in the family environment.

Focusing your family on God won't happen by default. I have spoken to countless families in crisis who tell me they have great intentions for integrating time with God into their family's daily routine, but it always gets crowded out. Good intentions don't get you anywhere. You must take the initiative to lead your family in seeking and connecting with God. Pro-activity is key. Consider what the author of 1 Chronicles wrote:

> *Search for the LORD and for his strength; continually seek him.* (1 Chronicles 16:11)

Do you have a daily prayer time at your house? How about a daily Bible study? If you aren't currently taking the time to focus your family on God, start thinking about how you can incorporate it into your schedule. If you don't have children, the best time to connect with God may be first thing in the morning, before you begin your day. If you do have kids and your mornings are consumed with rushing everyone off to school and work, maybe evenings would be better. You could create a routine of doing a small Bible study and praying together before bedtime. If you aren't in the habit of praying as a family, it may be a little awkward at first. Don't let that stop you. I like to say that clichés become clichés because they are accurate, and that's certainly the case for this one: the family that prays together stays together.

I understand this is easier said than done. You are busy, your spouse is busy, and your kids are involved in countless activities. There will always be a reason to let family prayer and Bible study slip through the cracks. But if you want to build a strong, flourishing family—a family that stays close through the years and can weather whatever storms come along—making God the priority is nonnegotiable.

At our house, we like to say, "Shoot for seven and be happy with five." In other words, our goal is to pray and study God's Word together every day of the week. But, you know as well as I do, some days it's just not going to happen. When the week is over, we consider it a success if we've hit the mark five out of seven days. God doesn't expect us to be perfect, but He does expect us to be earnest about building our family on the foundation of His truth.

Every negative issue that blows into your family will come as a result of not living according to God's Word—every single one. But if you will be faithful to put God first and seek Him daily, He will pour out abundant blessings. Remember Jesus' words:

> *Anyone who listens to my teaching and follows it is wise, like a person who builds a house on solid rock. Though the rain comes in torrents and the floodwaters rise and the winds beat against that house, it won't collapse because it is built on bedrock.* (Matthew 7:24–25)

You can't control the future of your family, but you can control the foundation it's built on. When you focus on God daily by engaging in prayer and Bible study as a family unit, you will build a house capable of standing through anything.

Be Quick to Forgive Your Family Members

Every family is made up of flawed human beings. You're not perfect; neither is your mother, brother-in-law or child. Since that's the case, you aren't going to get through life without being hurt. Not only will you and I have to deal with everyday broken promises and disappointments, but sometimes we'll face much deeper issues as well—problems with the potential to leave painful scars.

The second step to giving God first place in your family is to decide to forgive your family members of their wrongs quickly. Showing grace to one another and allowing for each other's mistakes is the oil that keeps the machinery of a family running. Without it, friction slowly builds to the point of burnout and disrepair. Refusing to forgive creates breakdown, but forgiveness brings new life. Consider Paul's words:

> *Be kind to each other, tenderhearted, forgiving one another, just as God through Christ has forgiven you.* (Ephesians 4:32)

Given the magnitude of what Jesus did on the cross, no grievance among family members is too big to be forgiven. While you and I were still wallowing in our sin, offending God in every possible way, He sent His Son to die for us—not after we straightened up, saw the light and apologized, but while we were still sinners (Romans 5:8).

Because God was able to reach out to us and offer us complete forgiveness even as we were hurting Him, we have a responsibility to do the same for our loved ones. Paul went into more detail in 2 Corinthians:

> *And all of this is a gift from God, who brought us back to himself through Christ. And God has given us this task of reconciling people to him. For God was in Christ, reconciling the world to himself, no longer counting people's sins against them. And he gave us this wonderful message of reconciliation. So we are Christ's ambassadors; God is making his appeal through us. We speak for Christ when we plead, "Come back to God!" For God made Christ, who never sinned, to be the offering for our sin, so that we could be made right with God through Christ.* (2 Corinthians 5:18–21)

In the same way that God brought us back to Himself through Jesus, we are called to offer forgiveness and reconciliation to those who have sinned against us. As Paul wrote, we are Christ's ambassadors. We can't be representatives of the forgiving grace of Jesus Christ and at the same time harbor unforgiveness against a family member. No matter how deep the wound, no matter how extreme the circumstance, we are called to forgive.

If you have been abused or have found yourself in some other oppressive situation where it would be unwise for you to connect directly with a family member, you don't have to. Seeing someone isn't a prerequisite for forgiving them. In your own heart, choose to release the anger and resentment you have for that person. The bitterness you are carrying isn't hurting them; it is hurting you. By choosing to forgive, you set yourself free from the bondage of what happened to you. Only then will you be able to move forward into a more complete future.

In less extreme cases, where family strife is the result of smaller issues, understanding your responsibility to forgive as Jesus forgives will make all the difference in mending your relationships and bringing your family back into fellowship with each other. Proverbs says:

> *Love prospers when a fault is forgiven, but dwelling on it separates close friends.* (Proverbs 17:9)

Again, you can't control what others do. You can't control what has happened in the past. But you can control how you respond. You can shape the future of the relationship by doing your part to forgive:

> *If it is possible, as far as it depends on you, live at peace with everyone.* (Romans 12:18 NIV)

Prioritize Quality Family Time

Quality time is essential to any good relationship. That's why the third step to keeping God first in your family is to make quality time a priority. Given the hectic lives you and I live, quality family time is something else that can easily slip through the cracks. Investing time in family members is essential to deepening these important relationships and keeping the family on course. Here are a couple of ideas to help you start working more family time into your routine:

- *Have dinner together several times per week.* Studies show that families that have dinner together three to four nights each week have children who are better adjusted and less likely to experiment with drugs or alcohol. Notice that it doesn't have to be every night. Sometimes meetings run late at the office, and kids have practices that lead to dinners on the run. That's okay. But as often as possible, sit down for dinner as a family. The dinner table is where true community is built.

- *Celebrate family successes and special occasions together.* In the Old Testament, whenever a family experienced a great blessing, they would build an altar to God. Usually, the altar was just a few stones piled together to commemorate the good thing that had happened. Every day, as they walked by it, they would be reminded of God's faithfulness. Jacob, the grandson of Abraham, did this with his family:

  > *We are now going to Bethel, where I will build an altar to the God who answered my prayers when I was in distress. He has been with me wherever I have gone.* (Genesis 35:3)

> Building an altar of celebration helped Jacob and his family focus on God and remember to put Him first every day.
>
> You and I may not want to build altars, but we can carry the same mindset into our own families by consistently celebrating successes and special occasions together. Make a big deal out of small victories in each other's lives. Celebrate significant moments. Birthdays, graduations, weddings and holidays are powerful times to reconnect with your family and focus on the blessings God brings.

These days, it's not uncommon for family members to be scattered all over the country or even the world. Still, geography doesn't have to hinder strong family relationships. Even if you live hundreds or thousands of miles from your family, you can stay almost as closely connected as if you lived in the same town if you put in the effort to make that connection a priority. Often, geographical distance makes relationships even stronger than they might otherwise be because family members learn to appreciate each other more. No matter where they are located, make a daily decision to honor your family:

> *Honor your father and mother. Then you will live a long, full life in the land the* L*ORD* *your God is giving you.* (Exodus 20:12)

In this commandment, God is speaking specifically about honoring your parents, but the sentiment can be extended to other family members as well. When you commit to honoring and deepening your family relationships by making quality time a priority, God will bless you with a full, loving family life.

LETTING GO

You and I have a responsibility to do our part to create Spirited-filled, God-focused families. But as we do, we have to simultaneously turn them over to God. We can build foundations, but we can't control outcomes. No matter how hard we work to point our kids down the right path or keep our relationships healthy, problems will come up, things will go wrong, children will turn away, and people will hurt one another. We can't mandate the choices our family members make, but we can choose to trust God in the midst of them. We can turn to Him when storms arise and ask Him what He wants to do in the situation. We can trust Him to rectify poor decisions and broken relationships. As we put God first and then let go and trust Him to work out His purposes, He will. In the process, He will build strong, beautiful families that display His grace and strength to the world.

CHAPTER 6

TEMPTATION

Winning the Battle Over God's Best

The essence of temptation is the invitation to live independently of God.

—Neil T. Anderson

God blesses those who patiently endure testing and temptation. Afterward they will receive the crown of life that God has promised to those who love him.

—James 1:12

Temptation is quite the chameleon. Taking on many different forms, it sneaks into your consciousness and aligns itself with your unhealthiest impulses and desires. For some of us, temptation comes disguised as foods we know we shouldn't eat. For others, it shows up as a pull to cross the invisible line into drunkenness. Some temptation hides out in our accountant's office at tax time or wraps itself in an opportunity to skim a little off the top of the company budget. Some temptation calls out as the need for one more high, then one more high, and then one more. One of temptation's most effective guises is sexual enticement. This temptation shows up in many ways, most commonly as a desire to have premarital sex, to view pornography or to step outside of marriage into an adulterous affair.

Temptation is not selective, and it's not something only a few of us face. We are all confronted with its advancements and titillations every single day. So, to be on guard against it, you and I have to be brutally honest about temptation's lure and how it manifests in our lives. What dangerous pull do you struggle with most often? Which of the temptations mentioned above resonates with you? If you think you stand above being tempted, you may be dealing with another temptation altogether—pride. No one is immune. In his letter to the early church in Corinth, Paul warned:

> *If you think you are standing strong, be careful not to fall. The temptations in your life are no different from what others experience.* (1 Corinthians 10:12–13)

Regardless of what is calling out to you and tempting you to stray, you can be sure you are not the only one. As intense as your struggle may be, it's not unique. In studying human nature and the Scriptures, I'm increasingly convinced that the devil only has about half a dozen tricks. He constantly throws those tricks in front of us because we seem to fall for them over and over. But we don't have to.

We will never wholly quell the raging storms of temptation, but we can discover how to stand in their midst. Remember, first and foremost, that being tempted is not a sin; it's just part of being human. The sin comes when you give into temptation and act on the impulse pulling you. But when you know how to resist the bait, you can avoid sin and all of its consequences. The goal, then, is not to stop being tempted but to discover how to stand against the temptation—or, to put it another way, to discover how to consistently choose God's best over the counterfeit pleasure at the center of temptation's ploy.

STANDING STRONG AGAINST TEMPTATION

If you spend any time reading or listening to national news, you know it's full of stories about people who went toe-to-toe with temptation and lost. There have been scores of headlines over the last few years about the indiscretions of prominent leaders in particular. Every single one of those indiscretions began with poorly handled temptation. As sensationalized as some of these stories become, they are all too familiar; they could be anyone's story. Even King David, whom the Scriptures uphold as one of the most revered and God-honoring men of his generation, committed a tragic sin because he handled temptation badly:

> *In the spring of the year, when kings normally go out to war, David sent Joab and the Israelite army to fight the Ammonites. They destroyed the Ammonite army and laid siege to the city of Rabbah. However, David stayed behind in Jerusalem.*
>
> *Late one afternoon, after his midday rest, David got out of bed and was walking on the roof of the palace. As he looked out over the city, he noticed a woman of unusual beauty taking a*

> *bath. He sent someone to find out who she was, and he was told, "She is Bathsheba, the daughter of Eliam and the wife of Uriah the Hittite." Then David sent messengers to get her; and when she came to the palace, he slept with her.* (2 Samuel 11:1–4)

David's downfall was the result of several poor decisions. First, David decided to stay home when it was customary for him to be at war. He wasn't where he should have been. If David had been on the battlefield with his men, he would have sidestepped the Bathsheba episode altogether. But as the old saying goes, "Idle hands are the devil's tools."

Second, when David noticed Bathsheba bathing, he had a clear choice to make: he could have turned away and refocused his attention, or he could've entertained Bathsheba's lure. Choosing the latter, he sent someone to find out who she was, taking a step closer to his downfall.

Finally, David decided to have Bathsheba brought to him. In doing so, he took definite action on his temptation and crossed the line into sin. The chain of events David ignited when he sent for Bathsheba resulted in tragedy and heartache for everyone involved, as all sin does.

David's affair is one of the most studied accounts in the Bible because it clearly illustrates the subtle interplay between temptation and sin. Even though David's temptation was sexual, his experience can be applied to any temptation we face. The indiscretion with Bathsheba highlights four critical steps you and I must take to find victory over every temptation that threatens to bring us down.

Step One: Admit When You Are Tempted

Before David's affair with Bathsheba, he led an exemplary life. As a teenager, he killed Goliath. Through his military career, he earned a glowing reputation and was highly respected. He rose to kingship in Israel. He even asked God if he could rebuild the temple in Jerusalem. A wealthy man, David donated his personal gold and silver to the building project. He reorganized the structure of the priests in the temple in a way that would remain the protocol for hundreds of years. How could this model of a man end up with such a black mark on his life? One of the contributing factors was likely that he was hesitant to admit such a thing could happen to him.

The first step to standing strong against temptation is to admit when you are tempted. Be honest with God and with yourself about what you are struggling against. Two primary mindsets keep people from admitting temptation. One is pride. The other is shame.

People who think highly of themselves and the positions they've earned in the world sometimes think they are above temptation's common lure. They believe they are exempt—that they are too bright to step into the traps that bring others down. Such a pride-infused refusal to admit temptation leads to a fall more often than not. Years after the Bathsheba incident, David's son Solomon wrote:

> *Pride goes before destruction, and haughtiness before a fall.* (Proverbs 16:18)

We will never know whether Solomon's wisdom regarding pride was connected to his father's indiscretion. Still, the proverb is true: when we are too high on ourselves to admit the possibility of sin or wrongdoing, we lower our defenses, and our chances for a catastrophe skyrocket.

The second reason most people are hesitant to own up to temptation is a sense of shame. They are embarrassed to admit the temptations they face to themselves, much less to God. Perhaps they feel guilty about the nature of the temptation, or maybe they don't want to take on the perceived weakness that comes with being tempted. But there is no shame in temptation. It doesn't strike because you are weak or something is wrong with you. It strikes because you are human. Temptation is an equal opportunity offender; it goes after everyone—and works especially hard on those who won't admit it's there.

> ***Temptation is an equal opportunity offender; it goes after everyone—and works especially hard on those who won't admit it's there.***

Denying temptation only makes you more susceptible to it. But when you admit that you are tempted, you open the door for God's power to work in your situation. He can only help you overcome your temptation to the degree that you express your dependency on Him.

Rest assured, when you admit your temptation to God, you aren't telling Him anything He doesn't already know. He won't be surprised. Be quick to lay everything bare before the One who knows you best and ask Him for His power to help you stand strong. As theologian John Owen wrote:

> *If we do not abide in prayer, we will abide in temptation. Let this be one aspect of our daily intercession: "God, preserve my soul, and keep my heart and all its ways so that I will not be entangled." When this is true in our lives, a passing temptation will not overcome us. We will remain free while others lie in bondage.*[5]

David learned this lesson the hard way. Later in life, well after the fallout of the Bathsheba incident, he penned the following psalm to the same effect:

> *Search me, O God, and know my heart; test me and know my anxious thoughts.*
>
> *Point out anything in me that offends you, and lead me along the path of everlasting life.* (Psalm 139:23–24)

As you and I navigate life's temptations, we would do well to admit quickly and keep these wise prayers on our lips.

Step Two: Recognize Temptation as a Spiritual Battle

We are engaged in a spiritual battle every day of our lives. When we acknowledge that reality, we are more prepared to handle the flaming arrows directed our way:

Stay alert! Watch out for your great enemy, the devil. He prowls around like a roaring lion, looking for someone to devour. (1 Peter 5:8)

We have an enemy who is hell-bent (literally) on destroying us. The devil schemes against us, tempting us where he thinks he can break us. He is constantly trying to get us to step away from the life God has in store for us and run after the carrot he's dangling in front of our noses. Every temptation we face is an attack in the ongoing battle he is waging. As Paul wrote:

For we are not fighting against flesh-and-blood enemies, but against evil rulers and authorities of the unseen world, against mighty powers in this dark world, and against evil spirits in the heavenly places. (Ephesians 6:12)

Since we know we are engaged in such a fierce battle, the devil's attacks should never come as a surprise. In a war, sneak attacks are one of the most effective methods of destruction. But since the Bible has already let us in on our enemy's tactics, we have the advantage of being able to sidestep surprise, as Principle II of Unshakable Faith tells us to do.

Unshakable Principle II: Sidestep Surprise

Even though temptation is a spiritual issue at its core, most temptation manifests itself physically. There's a strong physical component in sexual temptation; we were wired to be sexual beings. There's a physical element to gluttony; we were created with a need for food and with taste buds that signal enjoyment. There's a physical factor in every unhealthy addiction; once our body gets used to a particular surge of pleasure, we can become consumed by the drive to recreate that sensation again and again. But as we take on this powerful physical aspect of the temptations we face, we have to remember that it is part and parcel of the spiritual battle we're engaged in. The two cannot be separated.

Over the last several hundred years, one of the enemy's strategies for making us more susceptible to temptation has been his attempt to break this link between physical and spiritual realities. During the Enlightenment, French philosopher René Descartes outlined the first systematic argument for what has become known as the principle of mind/body dualism. He proposed that what you do with or to your body does not affect your mind, emotions or spirit. The ramifications of this theory have left us with a skewed understanding of the mind/body connection, which has resulted in an incorrect view of sin.

In response, countless philosophers, leaders of major religions and New Testament scholars have thoroughly debunked the dualistic argument. There is, they contend, a deep connection between your mind, your body and your spirit. As Dietrich Bonhoeffer wrote in *Creation and Fall: Temptation,* "Man does not 'have' a body; he does not 'have' a soul; rather he 'is' body and soul. Man in the beginning is really his body. He is one. He is his body, as Christ is completely his body, as the Church is the body of Christ."[6]

All you have to do is look at your life experience to know that your body, soul and mind are inseparable. I would venture a guess that some things you have done with your body in the past are still affecting your mind and your spirit. And you know from experience that what goes in your mind and spirit can affect you physically. God didn't create us as compartmentalized beings. He created us as three-fold persons—mind, body and spirit. Each of these three areas is intertwined with the others, and the spiritual battle is being leveled on all three fronts.

The devil wants to hurt you and me. He wants to hurt our loved ones. He wants to rob us of God's best, and temptation is his go-to trick. But God wants more for us. He loves us and wants us to experience the fullness of life. So when we find ourselves being tempted away from what we know is right, we must look to God and acknowledge that we are in the midst of a spiritual battle. When we can recognize our temptation as the tactic it is, we will be better able to overcome it.

Step 3: Steer Clear of People and Places That Tempt You

Sin doesn't just slip in and wreak havoc out of the blue. There's a process. Adultery, one-night stands, going too far, drinking too much, becoming addicted . . . these things are the result of thought patterns and small decisions over time. Often, they are the consequence of allowing ourselves to be around the wrong people or in the wrong places. David's disgrace with Bathsheba began the day he let himself lay out of work and look at a woman who wasn't his wife. Our biggest regrets usually start similarly.

God will give us the strength to stand against temptation, but He also hands us part of the responsibility. We have to protect ourselves by staying away from the people and places that foster temptation. We all know what those places are for us; we know who the people are. Instead of playing with fire and praying we won't get burned, we have to be mature enough to steer clear of flammable situations.

Taking responsibility means thinking several steps ahead. One of the wisest things you and I can do is build guardrails into our lives that make it difficult for us to be tempted and, if we are tempted, make it difficult for us to cross over into sin. Use common sense: if going up on the roof and looking at a woman bathing tempts you, stay off the roof. If going out with colleagues after work causes you to drink too much, don't go. If being online while you're home alone leads to viewing pornography, turn off the computer and do something else. If you're single and your friends have a habit of one-night stands, be more careful about spending time with them. The Bible warns to watch out for those whose minds are set on fleeting pleasure:

Instead of playing with fire and praying we won't get burned, we have to be mature enough to steer clear of flammable situations.

> *"Let's feast and drink, for tomorrow we die!" Don't be fooled by those who say such things, for "bad company corrupts good character." Think carefully about what is right, and stop sinning.* (1 Corinthians 15:32–34)

We get ourselves into trouble by justifying small, unwise decisions—sometimes out of desire and sometimes just out of convenience. For example, there may be nothing "wrong" with going to lunch alone with a coworker of the opposite sex, but if you are married, it's not the wisest decision. Maybe you really do need to discuss something important, but find another setting. A few "there's nothing wrong with this" lunches can quickly lead to a sense of intimacy between the two of you, spiraling into an emotional affair that paves the way for a physical one. I've seen the scenario play out countless times in different variations. The wise thing to do is to put a guardrail in place. In this case, decide you won't eat alone with anyone of the opposite sex other than your spouse under any circumstance. That way, you can head off the enemy's attack before it starts.

If you and I aren't careful, seemingly inconsequential decisions can put us on a slippery slope toward powerful temptation. Better to be overly alert and stay far from sin than to walk too close to the edge and get pushed over. This is not a game. We must do what we can to thwart the devil's schemes by making thoughtful, prayerful decisions about the places we go and the people we engage with daily. If we ignore the importance of these choices, we could be setting ourselves up for a major fall.

Step 4: Focus on God, Not the Temptation

A wise man once said, "What we see depends mainly on what we look for." The more you focus on the temptation in your life, the stronger that temptation will become. The more you focus on God, the stronger His power will become. Imagine how differently David's story would have turned out if he had gone back downstairs after he saw Bathsheba and turned his attention to praying and studying God's Word. But David focused on the temptation rather than on God and ended up stepping into a big pile of sin.

No matter how strong your temptation is, God is stronger. Not only that, He promises to give you a way out. Earlier in this chapter, we looked at Paul's declaration that the temptations you face aren't unique. Take a look now at how he finished that thought:

> *The temptations in your life are no different from what others experience. And God is faithful. He will not allow the temptation to be more than you can stand. When you are tempted, he will show you a way out so that you can endure.* (1 Corinthians 10:13)

No matter how powerful the addiction, no matter how great the attraction to the other person, and no matter how strong your craving for just a little more, God will show you a way around the snare looming in front of you. Focus your attention on Him. Then, when the way out presents itself, be quick to take it. Refuse to play the victim and claim that you didn't have a choice in your situation; you know that's not true. Paul was clear that God will not allow any temptation to be more than you can stand. He will show you a different path. You are not in this alone.

Perhaps you feel like you have already messed up, and no matter how much you focus on God, you can't undo the damage you've done. Let the end of David's story give you hope. Of course, David's sin with Bathsheba had consequences. The repercussions of sin can't be diminished (Galatians 6:7–9). But David learned from his mistake and decided to honor and follow God going forward.

When he reached the end of his life, David was living for God once again and doing great things for the kingdom. If you fast-forward hundreds of years to the New Testament book of Acts, David is described as a man after God's own heart:

> *David, a man about whom God said, "I have found David son of Jesse, a man after my own heart. He will do everything I want him to do."* (Acts 13:22)

Even if you have lost the battle with temptation in the past, and even if you are still dealing with the negative consequences of giving in, you can choose to start concentrating your attention on God and living the life He has in store for you from this point forward. Your past does not diminish you in God's eyes if you will look to Him for forgiveness and choose to focus your life around His truth now.

CHOOSING GOD'S BEST

Ultimately, all temptation is the temptation to trade God's best for something less. The devil tries to convince us that by giving in to temptation, we'll find what we are looking for. His scheme worked on Adam and Eve in the garden, and it still works on millions every day. When you and I say yes to what's tempting us and cross the line into sin, we trade God's incomparable plan for something that tastes good or feels good only for a moment. It's not a fair trade. We may experience fleeting pleasure, but we are left empty and craving more.

There's an ancient Cherokee legend about a young man who went to see the chief of his village. The young man said, "Chief, there is a battle going on inside me. In my mind, I see two wolves fighting. One wolf is evil. He's full of pride, lust, jealousy and greed. The other wolf is good. He's full of peace, love, humility and faith. They clash every day. Can you tell me which one will win?" The chief looked the young man in the eye and said, "The one you feed."

So it is with our ongoing battle between the devil's schemes to tempt us and God's best plan for our lives. If you ever get to the point where you feel overwhelmed by your temptation, you're feeding the wrong wolf. But as you cooperate with God by admitting when you are tempted, recognizing the spiritual battle you are in, steering clear of the people and places that tempt you and keeping your attention focused on Him, you will be doing your part to feed the right wolf. Then you will be able to stand strong during temptation's storms and be filled with peace, love, humility and faith.

CHAPTER 7

CAREER CHALLENGES

Getting from Where You Are to Where You Want to Be

Everything comes to him who hustles while he waits.

—Thomas Edison

Work willingly at whatever you do, as though you were working for the Lord rather than for people.

—Paul (Colossians 3:23)

I bet you started planning your career path from an early age. You had to. From the time you stepped into kindergarten, grown-ups began asking you what you wanted to be when you grew up. So you came up with an answer. I used to say I wanted to be a lawyer. Then I wised up and changed my answer to astronaut. What about you? What did you want to be? More importantly, do you want to be what you have become?

Most of us end up chucking our childhood plans somewhere along the way in favor of a career track that's wiser or more stable than being a rodeo clown. (No offense to rodeo clowns. Or lawyers.) The problem is, too often, we allow ourselves to get carried along by an erratic stream of monetary needs, personal connections and random job openings that sound interesting until we wash up on a shore we never saw coming. We may end up working a decent job but feel frustrated, out of sync or dissatisfied.

Whatever their form, professional storms are difficult to weather. If you feel like you are being tossed around by the current circumstances of your job or career, step back and evaluate what's going on from two perspectives:

1. Analyze your true **motives** behind the work you do. In other words, what definition of success drives you in the workplace?

2. Examine your **makeup** in relation to your career or job situation. How are you uniquely wired, and how does that mesh with the path you are on?

MOTIVES: HOW DO YOU DEFINE SUCCESS?

Your definition of success will not only determine your overall career path but also your daily performance on the job. If you define success by position, you'll be focused on advancing through the ranks of your company. If you define success by income, you may do whatever it takes, ethically or otherwise, to increase your bottom line. If your definition centers on power, you're likely to manipulate the people and situations around you in an attempt to gain control. If fame is your pinnacle, you'll devise plans to get your name spoken around America's dinner tables.

Since your definition of success drives your career—and since you probably spend anywhere from 200 to 400 hours working every month—it is safe to say that how you define success will shape your entire life. So what is success for you? What's your definition? Perhaps more importantly, how do you know if your definition is right? Is there a definitive measure? What if you continue pursuing your vision of success only to get to the end of your life and realize that you were off target all along—that your pursuit was empty?

As with most philosophical questions, the Bible can offer some insight here. First of all, Scripture tells us that success is not defined by the external measurements of society. Jesus warned:

> *Beware! Guard against every kind of greed. Life is not measured by how much you own.* (Luke 12:15)

Clear enough. But even though most of us would agree with that truth, we still live like our possessions are some sort of barometer. We think if we have more than everyone else—if we have the best, the newest, the most expensive toy/car/clothes/fill in the blank—we are successful. We win. But Jesus said that's not how life is measured. To discover more about breaking out of the trap of materialism, turn to Chapter 11.

Later in the New Testament, Paul gave us another clue to add to our working definition of success:

> *It is not that we think we can do anything of lasting value by ourselves. Our only power and success come from God.* (2 Corinthians 3:5)

The success we attain is from God, not merely from our efforts. As Paul was saying, success, as defined by human standards, is a skewed goal. It's not about us; it's not about what we can grasp. True success has a larger, lasting value.

Even though success will look a little different for every individual, certain principles inhabit all authentic achievement. Consider the three questions below. How you answer them is a good indicator of whether you are on the path to true success or whether a professional shift may be in order.

Question 1: Are You Serving Others?

Ralph Waldo Emerson wrote, "It is one of the most beautiful compensations of life, that no man can sincerely try to help another without helping himself." Emerson understood that helping others is good for your soul. What he may not have realized is that the level to which you are willing to serve other people will determine the level of your ultimate success.

The word *servant* is most associated with success in the Bible, but today, it sounds radical. You and I don't live in a culture that focuses on selfless service. Whether we like to admit it or not, our mindset is often one of, "What's in it for me?" The servant, on the other hand, asks, "What can I do for you?" He puts other people and their needs before himself and his own.

Jesus' disciples were as concerned with succeeding as we are. They even debated among themselves about which one of them was the greatest. They competed for recognition and accolades. They each wanted to be the guy to sit at Jesus' right hand in the kingdom of heaven. Jesus was quick to remind them that greatness and success are not about position but about service:

> *The greatest among you must be a servant. But those who exalt themselves will be humbled, and those who humble themselves will be exalted.* (Matthew 23:11–12)

In our quest for success, we have to cultivate the ability to humble ourselves and serve those around us. Significance isn't found in a salary but in how well we bless other people. For a deeper study on achieving true greatness through service, see my book *The Greatness Principle: Finding Significance and Joy by Serving Others.*

Question 2: Are You Growing Others?

Do your friends, family and coworkers feel encouraged after spending time with you? Do you respect other people enough to want them to reach their full potential? How you answer these questions will provide a glimpse into how well you are growing others. You and I have a fundamental responsibility to help the people around us become better human beings. As Goethe said, "If you treat an individual as he is, he will stay as he is; but if you treat him as if he were what he ought to be and could be, he will become what he ought to be and could be." How well are you helping the people in your life become what they ought to be and could be?

The best way to grow others is to take Jesus' most important command to heart and live it out in your day-to-day dealings with the people around you, a.k.a. your neighbors:

> *"You must love the Lord your God with all your heart, all your soul, and all your mind." This is the first and greatest commandment. A second is equally important: "Love your neighbor as yourself."* (Matthew 22:37–39)

When you choose to intentionally love God and love your neighbor as yourself, you cultivate good things in the lives of those you love. Plus, as you help others grow, God will grow you:

> *Give, and you will receive. Your gift will return to you in full—pressed down, shaken together to make room for more, running over, and poured into your lap. The amount you give will determine the amount you get back.* (Luke 6:38)

> ***Unshakable Principle VI:***
> ***Be a Willing Witness***

Take an interest in helping others in your life become better in every area. Show them love when they don't deserve it. Invest in their future. Support them in their spiritual journey. Remember Principle VI of Unshakable Faith and be a willing witness when they need to hear from you. The more you give, the more you will grow—and the closer you will get to true success.

Question 3: Are You Expanding God's Plan?

Success comes when you are more interested in doing God's will and accomplishing His work than doing things your way. That is, when God's plan for your life and your circle of influence takes the number one slot on your priority list. If you are wondering what God's plan is and how you can make it your top priority, refer back to questions one and two. God's plan is for you to serve others and help them grow.

Thomas Wolfe once wrote, "You have reached the pinnacle of success as soon as you become uninterested in money, compliments, or publicity." The best-selling author John Maxwell has added, "True success is obeying God." When you obey God by making His plan your motivation and then act on that plan by consciously serving others and helping them grow spiritually, He will make you successful in everything you do. If your definition of success is rooted in this truth, you will never have to worry about coming up empty in the end.

MAKEUP: WHAT KIND OF WORK ARE YOU WIRED FOR?

Once you have analyzed your motives in the workplace and defined true success, spend some time evaluating your makeup as it relates to your current work situation. In other words, consider how God wired you and how that wiring affects your career.

Gone are the days when people work in one profession or for one company for an entire career. In our culture, we are constantly reinventing ourselves. Our professional goals shift and evolve as our overall desires evolve. By taking the time to evaluate the skills, talents and abilities God gave you and what they are most suited for, you'll be able to choose your career more effectively and avoid some of the painful storms that come from being on a path that doesn't suit who you are. Begin by asking God to show you His wisdom:

> *If you need wisdom, ask our generous God, and he will give it to you. He will not rebuke you for asking.* (James 1:5)

Then ask yourself these four questions:

Question 1: What Does God Want?

You've probably realized by now that life is not about you. God's purposes extend far beyond your concerns. So it makes sense to ask yourself—and God—what He wants for your life. After all, He is the one who created you. He chose the parents you were born to, the country you were born in and the opportunities you had access to. He controlled all of these factors because He has a specific plan for your life. Ask Him what it is, and then listen for His answer.

Jim Collins, author of the New York Times Best Seller *Good to Great,* begins his masterful work with, "Good is the enemy of great."[7] You may be able to do lots of good things with your life, but if you are operating outside of God's will, you won't ever tap into the magnitude of the life He has in store for you. If you settle for good, you will miss out on great. God wants you to have the best, most abundant life possible (John 10:10). When you align yourself with His will, you will be able to do just that. To discover more about following God's will, turn to Chapter 3.

Question 2: What Are You Good At?

I grew up with a guy named John. John was a great golfer. He was wired for it. He played all through junior high and high school and then went to college on a golf scholarship. After college, he went on to have some success as an amateur. But John soon realized that he couldn't make a living out of the game he loved. So he examined the skill set he used on the golf course—the analytical way of thinking, the ability to predict outcomes, etc.—and concluded that many of those skills would translate well into the business world. He decided to get a degree in corporate finance. Now he uses the skills he was naturally blessed with to run a successful corporation.

God wired you to do something really well. What is that something? Try to find the point where your passion and your profession can cross paths. If you discover that sweet spot, you will be in a career you love for the rest of your life. Does your current work situation align with what you are naturally good at? Does your position allow you to do work you enjoy? Don't waste time doing something God didn't create you for. As Paul said:

> *For we are God's masterpiece. He has created us anew in Christ Jesus, so we can do the good things he planned for us long ago.* (Ephesians 2:10)

Question 3: What Is Right in Front of You?

God may ultimately have a different plan in store for your life, but He has put you where you are today for a reason. You have to be faithful and diligent to do what is in front of you.

He will place stepping stones in your path to get you where you are supposed to go, but only as you do what needs to be done right now. As the Bible says in Ecclesiastes:

> *Whatever your hand finds to do, do it with all your might.* (Ecclesiastes 9:10 NASB)

Paul echoed this sentiment later in his letter to the Colossian church:

> *Work willingly at whatever you do, as though you were working for the Lord rather than for people.* (Colossians 3:23)

God may be using your current situation to shape you into the person you need to be for the future. Whatever your work is right now, do it as if you were working directly for God rather than for other people, profit or popularity. As you do, He will guide your steps. If you are faithful in the small things, you'll be given more.

Question 4: What Is Your Life's Service?

True success is a byproduct of service. When you view your life and your purpose through the lens of service, the details of your career begin to fall into the proper perspective. Your life's work doesn't need to be centered on getting the best job, accomplishing all your professional goals and moving up the ladder but on continually seeking God's plan for your career and using that avenue to honor Him and love others.

Don't misunderstand: you can still land your dream job, strive for your professional goals and create lots of income. The difference is that, even as you do those things, they will not be your priority—they will not be the driving factor of your life. Instead, your success, whether small or great by the world's standards, will be the result of your service to others. The greatest leaders in every area of the working world are the greatest servers.

CHAPTER 8

ILLNESS

Uncovering the Purpose Behind Your Pain

A wise man should consider that health is the greatest of human blessings, and learn how by his own thought to derive benefit from his illnesses.

—Hippocrates

The LORD *nurses them when they are sick and restores them to health.*

—David (Psalm 41:3)

Your body is a carefully crafted machine. Just think about how much it does for you. Your heart beats over one hundred thousand times every day, pumping blood throughout your circulatory system and keeping you alive. Your lungs are made of fifteen hundred miles of airways that flood your bloodstream with oxygen as they whisk away carbon dioxide. Your nose is always on alert for dangerous chemicals in the air, while your ears are hard at work converting sound waves into nerve impulses sent to your brain so you can understand what you hear. Every detail of your body is a gift designed and given to you by the Creator.

In an ideal environment, every organ, muscle and molecule works flawlessly, each doing its part to keep you healthy and energized throughout your lifetime. But you and I don't live in an ideal environment. We live in a fallen world. Every day, we encounter stressors and deal with fallibilities—some self-inflicted, some we're born with and some simply a result of modern life.

While our bodies have been created with an astonishing ability to ward off threats and keep us healthy, illness is a reality we all deal with at some point. From colds, flus and migraines to chronic pain, dementia and cancer, we will all walk through some form of sickness and help our loved ones do the same. No matter what form it manifests in, illness is a storm with the potential and the tendency to shake us worse than anything else we come up against if we don't approach it from a place of unshakable faith.

THE DIAGNOSIS—STAGE CRITICAL

When I was only 45 years old, I was diagnosed with stage 4 colon cancer that had spread to my liver. One big, fast-growing tumor was found near the bottom of my colon, and seven other tumors (more politely called *lesions*) had nestled deeply into both halves of my liver.

The day before my diagnosis, I had visited my doctor because I had a nagging cough. Out of an abundance of caution, he suggested a chest X-ray. Now, I love my doctor, but I protested a bit. After all, it was just a cough. I had places to be. When he told me they could do the X-ray right down the hall, I gave in and waited the hour to get it done.

The next day, the day my world changed forever, was March 14—a day often referred to as Pi Day. Not Pie Day, as in, cut me a large slice of that delicious lemon meringue pie, but Pi, as in the mathematical 3.14—the first three numbers that are used to determine a circle's circumference (or something like that; it's been a while since I was in a geometry class). Anyway, on Pi Day, my doctor called and said my chest was clear, but the X-ray had gone just low enough to catch something that looked out of the ordinary on my liver—some suspicious lesions. He sounded somber, so I pushed him as to what they could be. He reluctantly told me that these lesions are typically a sign of something terrible, probably colon cancer. All I heard was C-A-N-C-E-R.

He went on to tell me that he had already made some calls and booked me that afternoon to see a brilliant young (my age at the time) oncologist who was building a practice in the area. My wife was able to meet me, and off we went. We got lost. We were nervous. I had cancer.

After a couple of hours with the oncologist, and some additional bloodwork and scans, it was clear: I had stage 4 cancer—*aggressive* stage 4 cancer. (I've always been an overachiever.) We had to jump on this immediately. An initial surgery was scheduled for the next week, with heavy chemo to follow. I was told that these early steps, if they worked, would probably buy me 10–24 months, with the hope being that a clinical trial would form or some new treatment breakthrough would happen during that time that could give me a year or two longer to live. Bottom line: not good.

To say that this diagnosis completely shocked us is the understatement of all understatements. I don't have a history of colon cancer in my family, or any cancers for that matter. For the three years before that fateful Pi Day, I had hit the healthiest arc of my life. My weight, a constant struggle, was finally under control. I was eating healthier. I exercised five to six days a week. I ran at least three miles every other day. Six months before my diagnosis, I had completed a Cleveland Clinic Executive Physical and had been deemed in perfect shape (well, almost . . . my vitamin D was slightly low, so over-the-counter vitamins were suggested). I must admit that when I heard the C word, sidestepping surprise (Principle II of Unshakable Faith) was not my first reaction.

I don't have the space to detail everything that happened in those early days. To make a very long story very short, I eventually had four major surgeries to remove the primary colon tumor and the seven liver tumors. Below, I'll tell you a little more about how those surgeries came to be. My oncologist referred to the approach we chose to take as *pushing the envelope*, a phrase I've now learned means "We'll almost kill you, but if you make it through, you might go on and live a long life." Two years later, by the grace of God and the medical intervention He provided, I was cancer-free. At the time of this writing, I remain cancer-free.

I may have won the cancer war, but I carry intense battle scars. I still have physical wounds to work through. My liver is cancer-free but not completely healed. I also have emotional scars I'm working on with my Christian counselor. Illness certainly leaves its mark on those it affects, but at the same time, it does the important job of directing our attention to the things that are truly most important. It brings focus. For me, walking through cancer burned away the chaff of what didn't matter for eternity in my life.

FOUR FUNDAMENTAL TRUTHS

Through it all, I discovered four fundamental truths we can all use to face storms of illness with faith and ultimately use them for God's glory. First, we must lean on God's power to strengthen us when we are weak. Second, we have to be willing to look for and live out the purpose contained in our sickness. Third, we must turn to God for our healing while cooperating with Him in doing our part to get better. Fourth, we must remember that this world's pain and suffering are temporary. Like everything else, they too shall pass. Let's look at each of these four truths more closely.

Lean on God's Power

Until a health problem strikes, most of us go through life feeling invincible. We think we have the world by the tail when we're strong and healthy. But when we find ourselves in unrelenting pain, stuck on a sickbed or hooked up to a chemo machine, we realize we are not indestructible after all. Even still, our first instinct too often is to face the challenge in our power. Whether because of pride or bad habits, we are quick to look to our strength before looking to God's.

If anyone in Scripture had the résumé and presumed strength to try to face illness on his own, it was King David. As a young man, David became famous for killing the giant, Goliath; in adulthood, he was an exceptional warrior; Scripture calls him a man after God's own heart (Acts 13:22); and David was the epitome of vigor, bravery and courage. But when illness struck, David didn't turn to his own capacities. He leaned fully into God as his source and his supply. Consider David's mindset in the following psalm:

> *Oh, the joys of those who are kind to the poor!*
> *The LORD rescues them when they are in trouble.*
> *The LORD protects them*
> *and keeps them alive . . . .*
> *The LORD nurses them when they are sick*
> *and restores them to health.*
>
> *"O Lord," I prayed, "have mercy on me.*
> *Heal me."* (Psalm 41:1–4)

Later in the Psalms, David continued:

> *I am suffering and in pain.*
> *Rescue me, O God, by your saving power.* (Psalm 69:29)

As accomplished as David was, he knew he needed to rely on God's power when he was suffering. You and I would do well to follow his example.

Being sick is nothing to hang your head about. Your weakness allows God's strength to be showcased. His power will work through you. Paul addressed this reality in his letter to the Corinthian church. About his own physical affliction, Paul wrote:

> *Three different times I begged the Lord to take it away. Each time he said, "My grace is all you need. My power works best in weakness." So now I am glad to boast about my weaknesses, so that the power of Christ can work through me. That's why I take pleasure in my weaknesses, and in the insults, hardships, persecutions, and troubles that I suffer for Christ. For when I am weak, then I am strong.* (2 Corinthians 12:8–10)

Paul's weakness ultimately made him stronger because it allowed God's grace and strength to be demonstrated. The same was true for me and can be true for you. When you are feeling under the weather, dealing with chronic pain or facing the uncertainty of the future with a disease you wish you didn't have, God's strength and power are available to you if you will turn to Him.

Live Out God's Purpose

When illness comes into your life, you can rest assured that God has a purpose behind it. Your job is to identify that purpose and choose to be a party to it. Remember Principle VII of Unshakable Faith: *Turn Pain into Purpose.*

> ***Unshakable Principle VII:***
>
> ***Turn Pain into Purpose***

God works everything together for the good of those who love Him (Romans 8:28). *Everything.* Even the painful, unwanted things become part of His plan for molding you into the person He wants you to be and readying you for the future He has in store. That can be hard to remember when you are facing another round of radiation, or the pain in your back won't go away, or you can't shake the flu you've had for weeks. But it's true. God knows the details of your situation; if you let Him, He will work those details together for your benefit and His glory.

So how do you let Him? What's your role? Here's how Jesus' brother James described your responsibility in turning pain into purpose:

> *Dear brothers and sisters, when troubles of any kind come your way, consider it an opportunity for great joy. For you know that when your faith is tested, your endurance has a chance to grow. So let it grow, for when your endurance is fully developed, you will be perfect and complete, needing nothing.* (James 1:2–4)

When you are tested, your endurance has a chance to grow. As it grows, you will become complete. Your pain can become the catalyst for developing you into your best self.

That growth won't happen unless you intentionally consider your troubles an opportunity for great joy. You must consciously decide to focus on the good in your situation. Your perspective plays a critical role in how your illness manifests itself, affects you and touches other people. Choose a spirit of joy. Be thankful for all the positive things that can come from your situation.

If you are having trouble identifying the positives, dig deeper; they are there. I encourage you to grab a pen and write down all the potential benefits of this trial. Could it strengthen your endurance, give you some needed downtime, help you connect with people you wouldn't otherwise know or grow your empathy for others with health challenges? Make a list of everything you can consider a positive.

Of course, there's another path you could take. It's a familiar path traveled by many people battling health issues. I call it the *Poor Me Path*. Instead of finding purpose and joy in your illness, you could choose to walk around with a cloud over your head, feeling sorry for yourself and angry that you are going through this ordeal. But I warn you: you will likely get sicker if you do that. Medical research proves as much. You will not be able to touch the people in your life who may be positioned to receive inspiration from your experience. And you will not grow into a stronger, more complete version of yourself. In short, you won't be able to receive the good that God wants to do in you and through you. The choice is yours.

> ***Unshakable Principle III:***
>
> ***Ask the Right Question of the Right Person Right Away***

Practicing Principle III of Unshakable Faith—*Ask the Right Question of the Right Person Right Away*—is essential to focusing on the positives and choosing joy. Too often, the reflex is to ask, "Why did this happen? Why do I have to go through this? Why does my friend/spouse/family member have to suffer?" But those questions drive you into a negative, victim-oriented mentality. Instead, ask, "What do You want to teach me through this illness, God? How are You going to use this pain?" When you focus on the good God wants to produce in you and through you, you will be happier, healthier and better able to cooperate with Him in bringing that good to pass.

One of the many incredible purposes illness has the potential to serve is to draw us closer to God. During my battle with cancer, my prayer life improved dramatically. I learned to pray for myself—something I had done too infrequently until that point. I also became intentional about praying for those going through the same difficulty I was. Often, while in the chemo chair, I would look up and down the aisles and pray for the others who were also undergoing chemo. I would pray for my doctors, nurses and medical professionals committed to helping me. I would pray for my family and for people in my church who were facing crises of their own. Learning to talk with God more regularly and in more circumstances throughout the day became a refreshed discipline I continue to practice and be grateful for.

In addition to deepening my prayer life, my illness taught me to make the most of every opportunity to seek and praise the Lord. The effects of my chemotherapy put me in bed for at least a couple of hours most days and early almost every night. I couldn't sleep but was forced to rest. During those long hours in the dark, I could have chosen to wallow in my misery. And believe me, there was plenty of misery to wallow in. Instead, I was determined to redeem the time. I didn't feel like reading or watching anything, but I could listen—so I did. I listened to far more podcasts, audiobooks, online sermons and wonderful hymns during that period than in the previous decade combined. Those countless hours of pouring good into my ears when there was nothing else I could do helped grow me through the struggle and drew me closer to God.

I have met countless other cancer survivors who have told me cancer was the greatest gift they ever received. Before my cancer journey, I was impressed with their perspective but a little doubtful. Now I understand and agree. The way this illness, or any severe illness, causes us to step back and reevaluate life is, in fact, a gift. Those who can see it as such have come to understand their struggle as a seed for the greater good. They looked down the *Poor Me Path* and decided to go the other way—to take James' advice, find the purpose in their pain and cooperate with God in living it out. Each one of them is stronger and more complete because of that decision.

Trust God for Healing

God is depicted as the Great Physician many times in the Scriptures. When facing an illness, our initial response should be to trust the Great Physician for healing—to turn our situation over to Him and say, "God, I may not understand why this has come into my life, but I know You have a reason. I give this illness/pain/struggle over to You. Help me see what You want to do through this time."

Then, as an act of faith, begin praying for healing. Ask your friends, family, church and coworkers to pray too. Calling people together to pray for you to get well is biblical. According to James:

> *Are any of you sick? You should call for the elders of the church to come and pray over you, anointing you with oil in the name of the Lord. Such a prayer offered in faith will heal the sick, and the Lord will make you well.* (James 5:14–15)

Chances are no one will be anointing you with oil in today's culture, but the point is clear: you and I need to pray for one another in faith and trust that God will bring His healing to every negative health situation we face.

Of course, we also have to cooperate with God in that healing. One of the traps we are conditioned to fall into is to use our faith as an excuse to ignore our responsibility for our health. God is clear that we reap what we sow (Galatians 6:7–9). That principle applies to our health as mightily as to anything else. If we sow physical well-being into our lives through positive lifestyle habits, we will be more likely to reap health in the long run. If, on the other hand, we sow unhealthy seeds into our lives through a low standard of living, we will eventually reap the crop for those choices too. You and I have been given a responsibility to care for the bodies we have been blessed with (1 Corinthians 6:19–20)—to fuel them with the right foods and to exercise them in ways that keep them strong. If we're honest, we could ward off many of the

> ***"Pray as though everything depended on God. Work as though everything depended on you."***
> ***–Saint Augustine***

problems we struggle with simply by making wiser choices regarding our health. For further study on what the Bible says about healthy living, visit www.BeUnshakable.com.

Still, while you and I should do all we can to avoid sickness and disease, that doesn't always mean our efforts will keep us healthy. We live in a fallen world, and our bodies are inherently broken. When illness strikes, we must deal with our new reality as it is, whether we played a part in manifesting it or not. Our job becomes cooperating with God for healing. How?

First, we should treat our bodies well and make common sense choices for our health in the face of our illness. For example, it's unreasonable to pray for God to heal you of lung cancer if you continue to smoke cigarettes every day. It's counterintuitive to pray that God will take away your high cholesterol, diabetes or the side effects of obesity when your daily food choices support and exacerbate those conditions. You must do your part. I must do mine. We are called to be wise stewards of our health. As we pray and trust God for healing when we're sick, we also have to go to work as our own health advocates. God has a lot to say about how to keep ourselves strong and healthy so we can accomplish all He has for us in this life. For a deep dive into God's plan for your health and wellness, check out my book *The New You: A Guide to Better Physical, Mental, Emotional, and Spiritual Wellness.*

Another way to cooperate with God for healing is to seek quality medical care. God works through modern medical practices every day. He is not anti-physician or anti-medicine. In fact, Luke, who wrote the Gospel of Luke, was a physician by trade. Luke traveled extensively with the apostle Paul after Jesus' death. And Paul, after spending time with Luke, was also known to suggest medicinal remedies. Consider what Paul wrote to his young friend, Timothy:

> *Don't drink only water. You ought to drink a little wine for the sake of your stomach because you are sick so often.* (1 Timothy 5:23)

Wine was commonly used as medicine in those days. Paul encouraged Timothy not to neglect a medicinal supplement that could help him feel better. In the same way, you and I shouldn't hesitate to use the medicines and tools of modern healthcare as we pray and trust God for healing. God can work through them mightily, as evidenced by my journey.

I mentioned earlier that the low end of my survival rate was predicted to be 10 months. Six months into my chemotherapy treatment, I had made little progress. The heavy chemo I was on had barely moved my cancer markers, and my tumors showed no signs of shrinking. With the clock ticking, Kelley and I began pursuing second and third opinions about my options.

Thankfully, some of the country's most excellent cancer treatment centers were within driving distance or a short flight from our house. We went seeking and searching. After one particularly defeating trip to a major cancer center, we were incredibly discouraged. I remember being in the hotel praying while Kelley did her best to catch up on all the sleep she had lost taking care of me. In a moment of faith, I confirmed my agreement with the apostle Paul, who said:

> *For to me, living means living for Christ, and dying is even better.* (Philippians 1:21)

I was ready to die if that was God's plan. I knew my eternity with Jesus in heaven was secure. At the same time, I wondered if I had more *living for Christ* to do. I opened my laptop and did one more search for my particular type of colon cancer. Several pages of clicks later, I discovered a surgeon who'd had some success with similar situations. He was in the Midwest, about halfway across the country from me. I called the next day to see about an appointment, only to find out that he had recently relocated and was now the head of a colorectal department at a major university hospital. The person on the other end of the phone wasn't sure what university hospital but promised to find out and call me back.

A few days later, I got an answer I could hardly believe. The surgeon I had become intent on tracking down was now the head of the colorectal department at the University of Miami, about one hour from my house! I booked his first open appointment and counted the days until I could get in to see him.

Simultaneously, I learned that Sloan Kettering Hospital in New York City had begun developing its first non-NYC liver treatment project at . . . wait for it . . . the University of Miami. I couldn't believe it. God was providing inroads to groundbreaking, innovative treatment right in my backyard. I booked the first open appointment with a surgeon in this emerging research department too.

God can turn things around in an instant. Within minutes of meeting with the renowned colon surgeon, he assured me that he could remove my tumor. Something many others had said wasn't possible or had told me shouldn't even be considered. The meeting with the liver surgeon wasn't quite as cut-and-dried. Seven tumors on the outer edges of what was still viable in my liver would be challenging to handle, to say the least. Once again, we talked about *pushing the envelope.* A treatment that had been successful two decades ago was now being modernized and showed potential for shrinking liver tumors. It was a stretch, but there was a possibility it could work for me.

So, after some serious coordination between the acclaimed colon surgeon and the aggressive liver surgeon, we had a new plan in place and a new sense of hope. The process was long and complex, hinging primarily on the four surgeries I mentioned earlier, but God worked mightily through the hands of these medical professionals and treatments to ultimately remove all the cancer from my body and restore me to health. Praise the Lord!

Through the prayers of many, and through dedicated medical professionals and advanced technology, God chose to work a miracle in my life. Yes, He is still in the miracle-working business. I must confess that I have no idea why He chose to heal me. It's certainly not because of my goodness or worth. As I fought my battle, some of my friends from the chemo chairs all around me lost theirs. Why did God work this miracle in my life and not in theirs? I will have to wait until all is revealed in heaven to find out. I can only say that

I am grateful. God chose, for reasons I cannot comprehend, to demonstrate His power in my life through an exception to the ordinary course of stage 4 cancer, showing that He is alive and still active in our day and time.

If and when God brings healing into your life or the life of your loved one walking through serious illness, be sure to give Him credit rather than merely crediting the new therapy, advanced technology or skilled doctor who may have been involved. God is the orchestrator and the ultimate healer at work behind all the medical treatment you receive. Or God may choose to sidestep treatment and heal you through an instant miracle, answered prayer, targeted nutrition and exercise or a combination of all these things (more on the ways God heals in the next section.) No matter how the healing manifests, it is not yours to take credit for. You have a huge responsibility to trust, pray, care for yourself and seek treatment, but God is the one who brings the healing. As David wrote:

> *The Lord nurses them when they are sick and restores them to health.* (Psalm 41:3)

Take Comfort in Eternity

So often, I get asked the question: *Will God heal me?* The conclusion I have reached in my research, and the greatest hope I can offer people who are suffering, is that, yes, God always heals in one of three ways:

Instantly. Sometimes God heals instantaneously, or at least very quickly. One of my fellow chemo warriors, a deacon of great faith that I met through my local oncologist, experienced such a healing from his colon tumor. He had a network of prayer warriors lifting him to God daily. On one scan, he had a colon tumor. Three months later, there was no tumor. I'd call that instantaneous healing. My oncologist, who grew up Hindu, now jokes that whenever he has a difficult case, he wants the pastor (me) and the deacon (my friend) to hold a prayer service. What a testament to God's power.

Slowly, through medical professionals and medical care. Often, God heals gradually through the dedicated work of medical professionals and the support of innovative, quality medical care. This form of healing is the most common and the most often overlooked. It's a journey I know well, as do many others who have bravely faced serious illnesses and now embrace full, vibrant lives.

In eternity. God always gives healing in eternity to those He has saved by His grace. That's why keeping His perspective on life and your illness's place within it is essential to being unshakable during the storm. Not all of us will be healed in this lifetime. For many, healing will come the moment we step out of this world into God's presence. As we walk through pain and suffering here and now, we must be careful to keep this reality in mind.

The illness you or your loved one wrestles with daily is nothing more than a blip on the radar screen in the context of eternity. It won't last forever, no matter how ugly or painful it is. So don't zoom in on it so closely that it's all you can see. Zoom out and see your storm and your entire life from a broader perspective. Look at this:

The dot represents your life, the number of years you are on this earth. The arrow represents eternity. Compared to eternity, your life and mine are like fleeting shadows. The Bible compares our lives to the morning fog—here for a little while and then gone (James 4:14). And while we are here, the trials we face are producing a glory for us that will last forever:

> *For our present troubles are small and won't last very long. Yet they produce for us a glory that vastly outweighs them and will last forever! So we don't look at the troubles we can see now; rather, we fix our gaze on things that cannot be seen. For the things we see now will soon be gone, but the things we cannot see will last forever.* (2 Corinthians 4:17–18)

If you are a follower of Jesus, your pain-free tomorrows will always outnumber your pain-filled yesterdays. That's a promise.

If you are tired of dealing with your illness, of living with the pain, of waking up feeling wretched every morning, know that a day of healing is coming. It may be in this life; it may not be until the next. But you can rest in the fact that the healing is on its way. Take comfort in what the book of Revelation says about the end of suffering:

> *He will wipe every tear from their eyes, and there will be no more death or sorrow or crying or pain. All these things are gone forever.* (Revelation 21:4)

Can you imagine the day that you step into Jesus' presence, and He wipes every tear from your eye? The words of the old hymn "What a Day That Will Be" sum it up well:

There'll be no sorrow there,
No more burdens to bear,
No more sickness, no pain,
No more parting over there;
And forever I will be,
With the one who died for me,
What a day, glorious day that will be.
What a day that will be,
When my Jesus I shall see,
And I look upon his face,
The one who saved me by his grace;
When he takes me by the hand,
And leads me through the Promised Land,
What a day, glorious day that will be.

To read more about facing death with strength and faith, turn to Chapter 14.

THE MAKINGS OF A MASTERPIECE

In the early 1900s, a mother took her young son to a concert hall to hear the great classical pianist Paderewski perform. While they were waiting for the concert to begin, the little boy slipped away and jumped onto the stage, where the shiny grand piano sat waiting to be played. Before his mother could react, the boy climbed onto the piano bench and started plucking out shaky single notes of "Twinkle, Twinkle, Little Star."

The other patrons in the concert hall—some indignant that this child would touch the master's piano and some stifling laughs—looked toward the mother to see what she would do. But just then, Paderewski walked onto the stage and approached the boy from behind. He bent down and whispered to the child, "Keep playing." As the little pianist continued to pluck away at the only song he knew, Paderewski stretched his arms around the child and began playing along with him. Suddenly, "Twinkle, Twinkle, Little Star" was transformed into a musical masterpiece that shocked and amazed everyone in the crowd.

When you and I give our struggles, pain and attempts to live well through diseases and sicknesses over to God, He works them into a beautiful masterpiece that demonstrates His strength and sovereignty. In the process, we grow up in His grace, have an indelible impact on the people around us and display God's faithfulness to His children. God made you; He knows your pain. He will carry you through and turn your greatest suffering into your greatest glory.

I will be your God throughout your lifetime—
until your hair is white with age.
I made you, and I will care for you.
I will carry you along and save you. (Isaiah 46:4)

CHAPTER 9

DOUBT

Keeping the Faith When Doubt Creeps In

The only limit to our realization of tomorrow will be our doubts of today.

—Franklin D. Roosevelt

Anything is possible if a person believes.

—Jesus (Mark 9:23)

My friend and colleague, Kerrick, had the unique experience of playing football at the college level. Many of the principles he learned during his years on the field at Furman University in Greenville, South Carolina, translate well into other areas of life—as lessons from the sports world often do. One of my favorite stories he tells deals with facing doubt. These are his words:

In early September 1995, tiny Furman University sent its football team, of which I was a member, to Atlanta to play the mighty Georgia Tech Yellow Jackets. This was the opening game for Georgia Tech—a top-25 team. It was going to be broadcast live up and down the East Coast on ABC Sports. The sportscasters were predicting a bloodbath. We were supposed to get crushed.

Before the game, our coach gathered us all in the locker room and told us to have faith that we could win. He told us we could have no doubts—that if we had doubts, we had already lost, and there wasn't any point in playing the game. He made us repeat, "No doubt, no doubt," over and over again until we believed that victory could be ours. We had been filled with fear, but he pointed us toward belief.

When we took the field that September afternoon in front of 70,000 people, plus the thousands watching on television, we had no doubt that we could beat Georgia Tech. And when we saw Georgia Tech run onto the field—when we saw how big they were—we still had no doubt. When we kicked off to start the game, and they fumbled the return, and we recovered, we definitely had no doubt. Then, when we drove down and kicked a field goal and went ahead three to nothing, we had no doubt whatsoever.

Even when they drove down the field and scored on the following kickoff, we still had no doubt. Then they got the ball back and drove down again to make the score 14 to 3. At that point, a little doubt started to creep in. Then they drove again and went ahead 21 to 3. The doubt was starting to mount. After they scored their eighth consecutive touchdown to go ahead 56 to 3, and it was still the third quarter, doubt doesn't even begin to describe what we were feeling.

Faith comes easily when our lives are going well. But when challenges start showing up, they can bring doubts with them. When we are down 56 to 3 in life, doubt often starts undermining our faith. It has the potential to really shake us. That's why it is so important to learn to stand strong against the doubts that would like to knock us around.

What kind of doubts do you wrestle with? Do you have doubts that are keeping you from taking steps in your career? Do you have doubts about relationships that cause you to put walls up around your heart? Do you have doubts about God that keep you from being able to trust Him?

If you and I let them, doubts will rob us of living the abundant life God wants for us. Still, avoiding them completely isn't an option. They invade our consciousness uninvited. So what can we do to keep doubts from taking control of our emotions and directing our actions? We have to learn to stand toe-to-toe with them, firmly grounded on a solid foundation of faith.

A COMMON CONUNDRUM

If you feel tossed around by doubts that won't go away, you aren't alone. Everyone, from the wisest spiritual teachers in our history to your closest friends and family members, has wrestled with intense doubts about the nature of God and their place in the world. Doubting is part of the human condition—especially when it comes to doubts about faith.

During Jesus' earthly ministry, He showed compassion to those who were quick to admit their doubts. One day in particular, Jesus and His three closest disciples, Peter, James and John, experienced a tremendous spiritual encounter with God on a mountaintop (read about it in Mark 9:2–13). But as soon as they climbed down off of the mountain, back into the valley of real life, they stepped right into the middle of a mess:

> *When they returned to the other disciples, they saw a large crowd surrounding them, and some teachers of religious law were arguing with them. When the crowd saw Jesus, they were overwhelmed with awe, and they ran to greet him.*
>
> *"What is all this arguing about?" Jesus asked.*
>
> *One of the men in the crowd spoke up and said, "Teacher, I brought my son so you could heal him. He is possessed by an evil spirit that won't let him talk. And whenever this spirit seizes him, it throws him violently to the ground. Then he foams at the mouth and grinds his teeth and becomes rigid. So I asked your disciples to cast out the evil spirit, but they couldn't do it."*
>
> *Jesus said to them, "You faithless people! How long must I be with you? How long must I put up with you? Bring the boy to me."*
>
> *So they brought the boy. But when the evil spirit saw Jesus, it threw the child into a violent convulsion, and he fell to the ground, writhing and foaming at the mouth.*
>
> *"How long has this been happening?" Jesus asked the boy's father.*
>
> *He replied, "Since he was a little boy. The spirit often throws him into the fire or into water, trying to kill him. Have mercy on us and help us, if you can."*

> *"What do you mean, 'If I can'?" Jesus asked. "Anything is possible if a person believes."*
>
> *The father instantly cried out, "I do believe, but help me overcome my unbelief!"*
>
> *When Jesus saw that the crowd of onlookers was growing, he rebuked the evil spirit. "Listen, you spirit that makes this boy unable to hear and speak," he said. "I command you to come out of this child and never enter him again!"*
>
> *Then the spirit screamed and threw the boy into another violent convulsion and left him. The boy appeared to be dead. A murmur ran through the crowd as people said, "He's dead." But Jesus took him by the hand and helped him to his feet, and he stood up.*
>
> *Afterward, when Jesus was alone in the house with his disciples, they asked him, "Why couldn't we cast out that evil spirit?"*
>
> *Jesus replied, "This kind can be cast out only by prayer."* (Mark 9:14–29)

Let's break the scenario down: A concerned father brings his son to the disciples for healing, but they can't do it. Their inability to cast the spirit out of the boy starts a commotion. The religious leaders begin calling the disciples fakes. Doubt starts to enter the picture, especially for the desperate father. When Jesus steps onto the scene, the father, hanging on to his last shred of hope, begs, "Heal him, if you can." That's when Jesus turns the situation on its head and teaches everyone an incredible lesson about doubt:

> *What do you mean, "If I can"? Anything is possible if a person believes.* (Mark 9:23)

Essentially, Jesus is telling the boy's father (and I paraphrase), "This has nothing to do with me; I can do anything. This has to do with your faith and with the doubt you are dealing with." To which the father candidly replies:

> *I do believe, but help me overcome my unbelief.* (Mark 9:24)

This father's simple prayer is one of the most powerful prayers in the Bible. While tinged with doubt, it is also full of faith.

As Jesus goes on to tell the disciples later in the passage, prayer was the key to the boy's healing. The only thing that could overcome the creeping doubt and open the way for Jesus to work was the honest prayer of that doubting father. With this passage in mind, consider the following realities about the nature of doubt:

- *It's easy to have faith on the mountaintop, but it's hard not to doubt in the valley.* When you are on the mountaintop with Jesus, feeling close to Him, and things are going well in your life, it's easy to have faith. But when you have to walk back down into the valley of everyday problems, doubt will do its best to sneak into your consciousness.

- *Doubt is a sign that there is a broken connection with God.* Intense doubt can signal that something is awry in your relationship with God. Let your doubt point you toward what needs to be fixed.

- *Doubt limits God's power in your life.* Consider how Jesus shifted the doubting father's perspective and made him realize that his doubt was preventing his son's healing. Jesus reminded the father, "Anything is possible when a person believes" (Mark 9:23).

- *Jesus only requires a small amount of faith.* Jesus knows that you and I will struggle with doubt. He knows our faith is imperfect. That's why He only requires a small amount of faith. He goes so far as to say:

  I tell you the truth, if you had faith even as small as a mustard seed, you could say to this mountain, "Move from here to there," and it would move. Nothing would be impossible. (Matthew 17:20)

  The father's prayer was colored with doubt, but it also contained a mustard seed of faith; that's all Jesus needs to see.

- *Prayer is essential to overcoming doubt.* Even though the father's prayer was imperfect, at least he was willing to pray. His prayer connected him with Jesus, and his faith paved the way for his son's healing. In the same way, prayer is essential to you and me overcoming our doubts.

DOUBT DRIVERS AND PRAYER

Every day, countless issues and situations have the potential to create doubt and drive that doubt deep into our hearts.

But, in every case, prayer enables us to stand confidently on God's truth. Keeping the above realities of doubt's nature in mind, consider these most common issues that open the door for doubt to creep in and the corresponding power of prayer to keep us firmly grounded:

Difficult Circumstances

When difficult circumstances cause doubt, prayer releases God's power into your life.

We've all known people who throw their hands up at God when the going gets tough. That's exactly what the enemy wants them—and you—to do. Whether you're facing an illness, a marriage that's falling apart, the death of a loved one, the loss of a job or any other circumstance you don't want to be in, Satan's first strategy is to start stirring doubt by getting you to question, rather than trust, God. He wants you to protest, "God, where are You? How could You allow this to happen to me? Why didn't You stop this?"

> ***Unshakable Principle III:***
>
> ***Ask the Right Question of the Right Person Right Away***

God has a different plan for your pain. He wants to use the difficult circumstances in your life to draw you closer to Him. He doesn't create the storms you face, but He does allow them. Why? So you will learn to trust Him and walk in His power. The pathway to that power is prayer. When you humble yourself before Him in prayer, God will give you peace and presence to help you deal with whatever you face.

When you pray, remember Principle III of Unshakable Faith: *Ask the Right Question of the Right Person Right Away.* Instead of demanding an explanation for how God allowed such difficult circumstances into your life, ask Him what He wants to teach you through those circumstances. No matter how things may look on the outside, He is working to turn your struggle into a victory.

Speaking of struggles, Kerrick and his football team didn't come back from the 56-3 deficit in their battle against Georgia Tech. Despite the pounding, Kerrick says that day's game was one of the most transformative of his football career. God used the adversity to bring the players closer together as a team. Thanks to the experience, they improved dramatically and ended up having a successful season. Even though they faced huge doubts—and even though circumstances didn't turn out how they would've liked—they got to the other side better for the journey. Isn't that how God so often works?

Intellectual Arguments

When intellectual arguments cause doubt, prayer reminds you of God's presence.

If you are a Christian, I'm sure you've encountered friends, family members, professors and colleagues who have tried to use intellectual arguments to call your faith into question. This is nothing new. Looking back to the scenario in Mark 9, that's precisely what the religious leaders in the crowd were doing: they wanted the boy's father and all the onlookers to doubt Jesus and His disciples, so they made intellectual arguments against their authenticity. Plenty of people still use the same approach. If you aren't careful, their cunning arguments can plant seeds of doubt in your mind and even cause you to question your faith.

These argumentative unbelievers fail to realize that Christianity is a faith of reason. Faith and reason don't conflict, and faith and science are not mutually exclusive. Faith, reason and science create a synergistic explanation for the world. Science and reason answer how things work; faith answers why.

No intellectual argument can produce doubt greater than your personal experience with God.

When you are faced with intellectual arguments targeted at shaking your faith, remind yourself that Christianity is intellectually defensible. Many of the greatest thinkers in human history have been, and are, followers of Jesus. And they have all understood that prayer is key to connecting with God's heart and overcoming the suspicions the world tosses around. Faithful prayer will remind you of God's real, active presence in your life. No intellectual argument can produce doubt greater than your personal experience with God.

Imperfect Christians

When imperfect Christians cause doubt, prayer helps you look past them to God's Son.

Many people let their faith get shaken when a Christian friend or acquaintance disappoints them. Again, this is nothing new. Think back to the father in our scenario. Doubt began to grow in his mind when the disciples weren't able to cast the spirit out of his son. He probably started thinking, *If they can't do it, they must be frauds . . . which probably means Jesus is a fraud.* When those associated with Jesus come up short, the tendency is to doubt Jesus Himself.

People who are not standing on a solid foundation will usually jump on any opportunity they see to use other people to cast doubt on Jesus. Why wouldn't they? If those associated with God fall, it makes their disassociation look all the wiser. Some people have let the child abuse scandals in the Catholic Church cause them to question faith in God. Others see an evangelist on TV they can't relate to and think, *He looks dubious, so this whole God thing must be dubious.* And, of course, countless people who are personally hurt or mistreated by a Christian—or someone claiming to be a Christian—turn their back on faith as a result.

Christians are human beings, which means they are utterly flawed. But Jesus is the perfect, sinless Son of God. Be careful not to let an imperfect person, an imperfect pastor or an imperfect church cause you to turn your back on a perfect Savior. Fix your eyes on Him instead of on the faulty Christians around you. They will always let you down, but Jesus won't. As Scripture says, you and I should be:

> *. . . fixing our eyes on Jesus, the author and perfecter of faith, who for the joy set before Him endured the cross, despising the*

> *shame, and has sat down at the right hand of the throne of God.* (Hebrews 12:2 NASB)

When you converse with God through prayer, you can see past earthly crimes and misgivings and focus instead on His beauty and perfection. If you put your faith in people, they will eventually let you down. The only person who won't let you down is Jesus Christ Himself. Turn your attention to Him and what He has done for you. Then the imperfections and flaws of this world won't be able to shake your faith.

Spiritual Dryness

When times of spiritual dryness cause doubt, prayer allows you to hear God's voice.

All believers go through periods of spiritual dryness, those stretches of time when you don't feel God's presence. You pray, but you don't hear His voice. You feel stranded in a spiritual desert. As one author wrote, "Any relationship involves times of closeness and times of distance. And in a relationship with God, no matter how intimate, the pendulum will swing from one to side to the other."

> ***Unshakable Principle VII: Turn Pain into Purpose***

During these times of spiritual dryness, doubt often begins to creep in. When you aren't hearing from God, it's easy to start doubting His love, plan and even existence. You may feel abandoned, but you haven't been. God will never abandon you. He has a purpose in the dryness. He wants to use the pain of it to draw you closer to Himself. He may even be preparing you for something big He has in store. When times of dryness come, make sure you stay connected to God through prayer, even if it is frustrating. That way, you'll be prepared to hear Him. Though you may feel like God is a long way away, continuing to pray will keep you nourished. As David wrote in Psalm 1:3:

> *They are like trees planted along the riverbank,*
> *bearing fruit each season.*
> *Their leaves never wither,*
> *and they prosper in all they do.*

See Chapter 13 to learn more about what can cause feelings of disconnection from God. For a deeper study of developing a healthy prayer life, visit www.BeUnshakable.com.

Recurring Sins

When recurring sins in your life cause doubt, prayer reveals God's grace.

Have you ever felt like you were locked in a battle with a recurring sin? You aren't alone. Believers all around you feel the same way. Consider what Paul wrote about his constant struggle with sin:

> *I don't really understand myself, for I want to do what is right, but I don't do it. Instead, I do what I hate. . . . Oh, what a miserable person I am! Who will free me from this life that is dominated by sin and death? Thank God! The answer is in Jesus Christ our Lord.* (Romans 7:15, 24–25)

The closer you draw to God, the more the enemy is going to try to throw you off course. The more passionately you live for Him, the more intense the struggle is going to be. But there is good news: as you lean into God through prayer, He will pour His power into your life to help you win the battle. And when sin does get the best of you, as it will from time to time, God will give you grace and forgiveness as soon as you ask Him.

These doubt-inducing issues will come into your life at some point. When they sneak in and start trying to tempt you to question your faith, remember the possessed boy's father from Mark 9. As he did, choose to have enough faith to ask Jesus for help. Be willing to say, "I do believe, but help me overcome my unbelief." Those words can release God's power in your life. As you learn to move forward in prayer through every situation that blows doubt your way, you will be able to stand with tested, unshakable faith in the face of life's harshest storms.

CHAPTER 10

PARENTING CHALLENGES

Unlocking the Keys to Success with Your Kids

Parents are the ultimate role models for children. Every word, movement, and action has an effect. No other person or outside force has a greater influence on a child than the parent.

—Bob Keeshan (Captain Kangaroo)

A house is built by wisdom and becomes strong through good sense.

—Proverbs 24:3

Parenting is one of the greatest joys we can experience on this side of heaven. But it's also a journey filled with trials and transformations that often leave us questioning if we're doing it right. Parenting challenges begin the day you bring a baby home. I will freely admit that the day Kelley and I brought Alex home from the hospital, I had no idea what I was doing. As you may have guessed, he didn't come with an instruction manual. And neither do your children. From day one, our joys and triumphs as new parents run parallel with the obstacles we all face as we learn to navigate this crucially important role.

Parenting challenges may change over the years, but they will always be there. The cute little baby you hold in your arms becomes a tantrum-throwing three-year-old. The innocent, loving six-year-old who thinks you are a hero morphs into a teenager whose lingo and clothing you don't quite understand. Then, before you know it, that teenager heads off to college, leaving you to grapple with the delicate balance of continuing to guide while letting go.

At the start of this journey, many of us believe that, like the Beatles said, "all you need is love." Toss in some practical advice, and it should all fall into place, right? But as reality sets in, we quickly discover that successful parenting requires so much more. We need wisdom, not to mention a blueprint for how we can best raise children in the way they should go. Scripture reminds us:

> *A house is built by wisdom and becomes strong through good sense.* (Proverbs 24:3)

Healthy families don't happen by accident. They are the result of intentional, wise decisions made by parents who understand the power of their role—not as perfect parents, but as prudent ones committed to raising their children to be individuals of character who know God, love Him and reflect Him well in their lives. As we explore these keys, I want to credit several role models I had for successful parenting, from my own parents to other mentors and teachers from whom I learned along the way.[8]

KEYS TO UNSHAKABLE PARENTING

Whether you're navigating life as a new parent, in the throes of the early school years, striving to connect with a rebellious teenager or trying to repair a strained relationship with an adult child, remember this: you can build a healthy family without doing everything exactly right. You can take steps to set the stage in a way that will equip you well to handle any parenting challenge you encounter in the years to come. God gives immense grace in this area where we all want to succeed but so often feel like we fall short. We need to grant ourselves a similar measure of grace as we do all we can to follow God's prescription for raising our children well and walking with them amidst the storms that will inevitably blow around us. When we search the Bible for guidance in this area, four key unshakable principles rise to the top:

1. Prepare your children for life.
2. Provide protection in life's storms.
3. Point your children to God.
4. Pray for your children every day.[9]

Let's look at each of these key elements in detail.

Prepare Your Children for Life

One of the primary goals of parenting is to prepare your children for life. God designed the family to be the training ground for life's essential lessons. Children learn skills from you that they won't pick up anywhere else: how to walk, talk, eat and relate to others, to name a few. Even modern necessities like navigating technology are learned in the context of the home environment. But, as wise parents, we know that our responsibility to prepare our kids for life stretches far beyond the practical. Look at Luke's words concerning how Jesus grew during His years at home.

> *Jesus grew in wisdom and in stature and in favor with God and all the people.* (Luke 2:52)

This verse identifies four important areas of development that we should be aware of beyond the practical necessities of life.

1. Jesus grew in wisdom (mental growth).
2. Jesus grew in stature (physical growth).
3. Jesus grew in favor with God (spiritual growth).
4. Jesus grew in favor with people (social growth).

Be creative in thinking through how you can help your children grow mentally. Spark their curiosity and encourage them to think deeply and read enthusiastically. Be intentional about giving them what they need to grow strong and healthy physically, especially given modern culture's propensity for junk foods and inactive lifestyles. Make sure you are connected to a church family where they can grow spiritually in addition to providing an environment for spiritual growth at home. Provide ample, varied opportunities for them to connect with others and develop socially. Combining thoughtful, directed training in these areas with life's everyday practical lessons will put your children on the path to being well-rounded, resilient individuals.

As your children grow and mature in all these ways, three aspects of their preparation are fundamental for you to lean into. Volumes have been written about all three, and I obviously can't cover everything in these pages. Still, it's well worth highlighting these crucial elements to focus on with your children while you have the time: healthy relationships, godly values and biblical character.

- **Healthy Relationships**
  Your child's happiness will be determined mainly by the relationships they create. As we all know, relationships don't just happen. They are built over time on the foundations of truthfulness, honesty and vulnerability. These things must be modeled at home so our kids can mirror them in their own lives. How you interact with your spouse, neighbors, friends and others will leave a lasting impression on your children.

- **Godly Values**
  Whether you realize it or not, your children are constantly absorbing messages about what you value most. They observe how you handle work, time, money, friendships, and your relationship with God. Kids are smart; they notice when your actions don't match your words. They understand that, regardless of what you claim is important, it's your behavior that reveals your true values. The values you model in your own life resonate far more than any lecture you could give.

- **Biblical Character**
  Your child's character will develop at home. It's shaped by the choices you make and the habits you establish. Good character grows from consistently doing the right thing and through reading and memorizing Scripture. Character is more caught than taught. So if you want your children to embrace traits such as honesty, kindness, and integrity, they must witness these qualities in you every single day.

The Bible clearly states that parents are responsible for preparing children for life—not the government, teachers, coaches or friends in the community. While all those others play important roles over the years, raising your kids in the right way (Proverbs 22:6) is your responsibility. If you don't teach your children about relationships, character and values, the world will fill in the gaps, often with lessons you disagree with.

As a mentor memorably reminded me once, the moment you took part in conception, you received a job description. Part of that job description is outlined in this verse:

> *You must commit yourselves wholeheartedly to these commands that I am giving you today. Repeat them again and again to your children. Talk about them when you are at home and when you are on the road, when you are going to bed, and when you are getting up.* (Deuteronomy 6:6–7)

Some parents hesitate to teach their children about God, saying, "I'll let my child decide for himself when he's older."

But this approach can send the wrong message—that God and faith are optional. Children need guidance and structure to develop strong values, especially in a society that often blurs the lines between right and wrong. You are hurting your kids if you say that God is an option. As long as they are under your roof, you are responsible for setting boundaries, sharing your faith and guiding them toward truth. Doing otherwise in the name of "letting them choose" is abdicating your responsibility as a parent. Yes, someday they'll make their own decisions, but for now, you can prepare them well by laying a foundation that will last a lifetime. For recommended parenting resources, visit www.BeUnshakable.com.

> ***Unshakable Principle I:***
> ***Secure a Solid Foundation***

Provide Protection in Life's Storms

Have you ever been caught outside in a sudden storm? In those moments, all you want is to find a place of refuge—a spot to escape the pounding rain and whipping winds, somewhere warm and peaceful.

Life's storms are no different. Whether they come as emotional struggles, physical hardships or relational conflicts, we all need a safe place to run to. For our children, home should be the place of refuge. Look at these words from Scripture:

> *Those who fear the LORD are secure;*
> *he will be a refuge for their children.* (Proverbs 14:26)

Part of God's design for the family is to be that refuge—a haven where children feel safe, loved and supported, even when life feels chaotic. That's why the second key to successful parenting is to ensure that you're providing protection in the inevitable storms of life, not to shield children from every challenge but to equip them to navigate the obstacles.

Notice the keyword here: provide protection *in* life's storms, not *from* life's storms. We live in a world where problems are real, challenges are unavoidable and storms—both literal and metaphorical—are a part of life. As parents, we can't (and shouldn't) protect our kids from every storm that whips up around them. Instead, our goal should be to provide them safety, guidance and strength through the storms. It's not about creating a storm-free life but preparing them to weather the inevitable.

Storms come in many forms, and every storm carries its unique challenges. Here are three common storms every family will likely face at some point:

1. *The Storm of Rejection*
   Rejection is one of life's most personal and painful storms. Rejection can leave deep scars, whether it's being excluded by friends, not making the team or facing heartbreak. While rejection hurts, it's also an opportunity for growth. As parents, we can create a safe space for our kids to process these experiences. Instead of trying to fix the situation, sometimes the best thing we can do is validate their feelings, remind them of their worth and help them see that rejection isn't the end—it's part of life's journey.

2. *The Storm of Change*
   Change is inevitable. Relationships shift, jobs end, addresses change and life moves on, often before we're ready. Whether positive or negative, change can be stressful, especially for children. How can you protect your kids in this storm? By being their constant in a world of uncertainty. Skip the lectures or lengthy stories about your own experiences. Instead, listen. Let your kids talk about their fears and frustrations. Listening shows them your love. And knowing they can talk to you creates a sense of stability amidst the chaos of change.

3. *The Storm of Failure*
   No one wins all the time. Tests are failed, shots are missed and relationships fall short. Failure can feel crushing, but it can also be an influential teacher. As parents, we can't prevent our kids from failing, but we can turn those failures into opportunities for growth. Make home a safe place where they learn that failure isn't final—it's a launchpad for the next big thing. Teaching children to handle failure in the secure environment of the family will prepare them for the inevitable failures that will come during harsh realities later in life. Let your kids know that they're never alone in their failures. Be there to encourage, guide and help them see the lessons hidden in their setbacks.

No matter what storm your family faces, the good news is that, with God's help, you can protect your kids during it. Remember, your role isn't to remove every obstacle from your child's path but to equip them with the faith, resilience and wisdom they need to walk through the challenges. By being a steady presence in their lives—a place of refuge—they'll learn to trust God, face life's storms with courage and emerge stronger on the other side.

Point Your Children to God

The most essential thing we can teach our children is how to know and love God. Parenting, at its core, is about pointing our kids to Him. Yet, if we're honest, the thought of nurturing our children's faith can feel overwhelming. For some, the idea of not having all the answers is enough to stop us in our tracks.

But let me encourage you with this: you don't need to have all the answers. You won't. If you haven't realized that yet, you will soon enough. Your kids' questions will quickly outpace your understanding, and that's okay. Children's curiosity may start small with questions like, "Why is the sky blue?" or "Why do dogs bark?" These can be answered with a bit of creativity or a quick Internet search. But as your children grow, their questions will deepen:

- "How do I know there is a God if I can't see Him?"
- "If God is good, why is there evil and suffering?"
- "If God is in control of everything, why did God allow Grandma to die?"

These are tough, heart-wrenching questions that don't come with easy answers. And as parents, we must humbly admit that our understanding is limited. But here's the good news: we serve a God who does have the answers. While we may be unable to explain every mystery of life, we can point our children to the One who knows everything. As mentioned earlier in this chapter, that's our most important role as parents—to guide our kids toward God. This has always been the case and always will be. Note how Paul encouraged the Christian parents in Ephesus to raise their children:

> *Bring [your children] up with the discipline and instruction that comes from the Lord.* (Ephesians 6:4)

This isn't about being perfect parents or having all the theological answers. It's about authentically walking alongside our children as fellow learners, students of Scripture and followers of Christ. How can we best do this? Consider these two ways:

1. *Model a life of authentic faith.*
   There's definite value in structured teaching—sitting down with your children to read the Bible, pray and discuss God's truth. These intentional moments help lay a foundation for their faith and should be part of your family's routine. However, how we live our lives speaks louder than formal teaching. Children learn the most by watching us. Like character, faith isn't just taught—it's caught. Our children will absorb what we genuinely believe based on how we live. Our example becomes their guide.

- Do they see us worshipping and honoring God in our daily lives?
- Do they see us turning to God when life gets tough?
- Do they see us praying for God's will and direction when we don't know what to do?
- Do they see us prioritizing church and community with other believers?

If our kids don't see these habits in our lives, why should they embrace them on their own? When we face financial struggles, grief or pain, we have an incredible opportunity to show our kids where our strength comes from. If they see us leaning on God during life's storms, they'll learn that His promises are real and reliable. If they see us reading our Bibles, they'll understand the importance of grounding their lives in Scripture. If they see us making church a priority, they'll recognize the value of worship and fellowship with other believers. On the other hand, if we try to handle everything on our own and neglect church for different activities, they may grow up thinking faith is unnecessary or irrelevant.

The responsibility we have as parents to model faith is both humbling and inspiring. Again, we don't have to be perfect, but we do need to be authentic. Our kids need to see us striving to grow in our relationship with God, even when we stumble. They need to see us asking for forgiveness when we fall short and leaning on God's grace every step of the way.

2. *Teach children to lead a life that is accountable to God*
   While we have been given authority over our children as their parents, they are ultimately accountable to their heavenly Father, not us. One of the greatest gifts you can give your children—and one of the things that will help you circumvent many parenting challenges along the way—is to remind them early and often of their accountability to the God who loves them. As you do, they will begin to realize that He is with them in every situation and that, as they go through their days, they are accountable not just to you but to Him. When instilled early, this principle shapes how they live and helps them navigate life's decisions with an eternal perspective.

> ***One of the greatest gifts you can give your children is to remind them early and often of their accountability to the God who loves them.***

Helping kids understand this kind of accountability begins with teaching them to see that their decisions—how they behave, the choices they make, the company they keep—are ultimately between them and God. He sees everything they say and do. Every choice they make is either an offering of worship or a rebellion against Him. They don't escape His presence when they scroll social media, head out on a date, walk into a party or go off to college. When children understand that they are always in God's presence, not only do they feel secure and grounded, but they also develop a moral compass that extends far beyond parental oversight.

Teaching this accountability is not about control but about connection. It connects your children to the God who loves, guides and wants the best for them. It teaches them to trust His authority and embrace His unceasing presence in their lives. In doing so, it helps them walk confidently into the future, knowing they are seen, held and loved by the One who created them.

Once again, be careful to remember that, as parents, we must live this out ourselves. Children are quick to discern hypocrisy. If we teach them to acknowledge their accountability to God but fail to model that accountability in our lives, our teaching will ring hollow. Do you recognize a theme here? We must embody what we wish to instill, showing children through our actions that God is our ultimate guide and authority.

Pray for Your Children Every Day

As flawed human beings, we are bound to be imperfect parents. We will make mistakes and stumble; that goes with the territory. However, the good news is that we are not in this alone. God gave us our children and loves them even more than we do. He wants to work in their lives, guiding and protecting them, and revealing Himself in and through them. The single best way we can invite Him to saturate their lives for His glory is by committing to pray over our children. Here are four simple yet powerful ways to pray for your children every single day:

1. *Pray for your children to have a personal relationship with Jesus.* Until your children come to know Jesus personally, pray for their salvation. Pray that their hearts, minds and eyes will be open to His truth and that they will desire a relationship with Him from a young age. If you have older or adult children who have never accepted Jesus as their Savior, pray for them similarly—do not give up (Matthew 7:7). Pray that God will work in their lives and reveal Himself in a way that will lead them to a relationship with Him. Nothing is more important than praying for the salvation of your children.

2. *Pray for God's protection for their developing hearts and minds.* Our most urgent prayers for our children are usually for their protection—and with good reason, given our tumultuous world. While we generally think of protection prayers concerning physical safety, let me also encourage you to pray for your children's spiritual, mental and emotional protection. Pray that their hearts and minds would be guarded from seeds the enemy would like to plant that could take them away from God's best. Pray that no weapon formed against them, in any realm of their lives, would be able to prosper (Isaiah 54:17).

3. *Pray for a growing love of God's Word.*
   A passion for the Word of God, the Bible, will be essential for our children to walk in His way throughout their lives. This will, in turn, help them weather the storms they'll face. Pray that they will have a deep desire to know and be filled with God's truth, allowing it to be their first source and final authority all the days of their lives. When they are young, read key Bible stories to them and teach them about the Life of Christ. As they grow, ensure they learn to study and search the Scriptures for themselves.

4. *Pray for your children to follow God's will.*
   As your children grow, pray diligently that they will seek God's direction for their lives. Pray that they will lean into His guidance as they make the choices that will shape who they are becoming. Pray that God will continually lead them along the paths He wants them to travel, growing them into the men and women He desires them to be. Just as the Lord's Prayer (Matthew 6:9-13) instructs us to pray daily for God's will to be done in our lives, let's also pray for God's will to be done in the lives of our children. As long as your child is in the center of God's will, everything will be OK.

I'll say it one last time: you don't need to be a perfect parent. There is no such thing. But if you will commit to being a praying parent who prepares their children for life, protects them in storms and points them toward God, you will be doing your part to provide the strongest possible foundation for lives well lived. You will be preparing both yourself and your children to be unshakable, together and individually, no matter what comes your way.

A Lasting Parental Legacy

Parenting is one of God's most extraordinary callings in life and also one of the hardest. However, it's in the everyday moments—reading a Bible story at bedtime, praying together over a tough decision, attending church together and comforting your child with God's promises—that you leave a lasting spiritual legacy.

As you walk this journey of faith, remember that God equips those He calls. He will provide you with the wisdom and strength needed to guide your children toward Him. Live your life in such a way that your kids want to follow your example—not because you've got it all together, but because they see the light of Christ in you. Trust God, point your children to Him, and watch as He works in their hearts in ways you could never imagine.

As you navigate the challenges that parenting presents, always remember this: God's wisdom is your greatest tool. Seek His guidance daily, and you will find the strength and clarity needed to stand strong.

CHAPTER 11

FINANCIAL STRESS

Discovering the Secret of Openhanded Living

My problem lies in reconciling my gross habits with my net income.

—Oscar Wilde

If you are untrustworthy about worldly wealth, who will trust you with the true riches of heaven?

—Jesus (Luke 16:11)

Dream with me for a minute. No matter what financial storm you are facing right now, let yourself imagine a reality where you don't live with constant stress over money, you don't struggle to make ends meet each month, you are completely out of debt, you aren't a slave to consumerism and materialism, you can save for the future, and you have the desire and ability to be generous with people in need and causes beyond your immediate concern. Sound like a nice way to live? It's possible. In fact, this is the way God wants your financial life to look.

Unfortunately, you and I—along with the vast majority of Americans—have grown up with a skewed understanding of money and possessions. Based on misinformation, poor examples and our personal desires, we have developed a certain paradigm for understanding and managing our income, a paradigm that has gotten us into a lot of trouble. Our collective wrong perspective has led us into seemingly insurmountable debt, broken apart our families and caused high levels of stress and anxiety. Our intentions to handle our resources well may be good, but money in our culture has gone bad.

You may have heard the famous quote, "We buy things we don't need, with money we don't have, to impress people we don't even like." Have you ever been there? Money has become a way of keeping score. It's as if we are competing to see who can get the most stuff, live in the biggest house and wear the most expensive clothes. No matter how much we have, we always seem to need more. Financial stress is a shadow that never leaves us alone.

Most of our money problems boil down to bad financial decisions that are the result of our distorted perspective. We are usually so rooted in our understanding of money management (or mismanagement) that we don't even realize we are making poor decisions. Like fish in water, we can't see the reality of the environment around us. We are just doing what we know to do and wondering why we continually live under the thumb of financial oppression. In our desperate search for security and status, we reach for all we can, and when we get it, we hold on tightly.

OPENHANDED LIVING

Have you ever heard how monkey hunters catch their prey? Long ago, an insightful hunter in India figured out that monkeys are selfish little creatures, so he came up with a way to capture them that takes advantage of their nature.

First, the hunter cuts a small hole in one end of a coconut—just big enough for the monkey to squeeze his hand into—and ties a long cord to the other end. Then, he sprinkles peanuts, banana chunks or some other treat into the hole, places it in the monkey's path and sneaks away, holding the other end of the cord, to watch his plan unfold.

Inevitably, an unsuspecting monkey comes along, sniffs out the treat, inspects the container and then wriggles his little hand into the hole to grab the treasure. With that, the hunter's job is done. All he has to do is yank his side of the cord, and the whole monkey/coconut kit and caboodle lands at his feet.

Why wouldn't the monkey pull his hand out of the coconut and run for his life? Because once a monkey gets his hand on something he wants, he won't let go. And with his fist wrapped around the goods, he can't get his hand back out of the hole. He could save himself if he would just loosen his grip, but he clings tightfisted to what's his. As a result, he's trapped.

It's easy for you and me to see how ridiculous the monkey is being. If we were sitting at the edge of the jungle watching the scenario play out, we would scream, "Let go! What's in your hand isn't worth your life!" And yet, back in our corner of the world, we are as guilty as the monkey. We hold on too tightly. We want what is ours, and we want it so badly that we're often blind to the consequences of our grasping.

But is what we have our hands wrapped around even ours? In the New Testament, James says:

> *Whatever is good and perfect is a gift coming down to us from God our Father, who created all the lights in the heavens.* (James 1:17)

Everything good in our lives comes from God. Paul echoed James' words and took things a little further:

> *Teach those who are rich in this world not to be proud and not to trust in their money, which is so unreliable. Their trust should be in God, who richly gives us all we need for our enjoyment.* (1 Timothy 6:17)

Notice Paul's assertion that God gives us all we need. We may have worked hard for the money that has come into our lives, but God has given us the breath, health, strength and intelligence to do our jobs. He has given us the ability to earn a living. And He has made us responsible for providing for our family and saving for the future.

Furthermore, God gives us what we need for our enjoyment. God wants us to live a blessed life. He wants us to have fun. There is absolutely nothing wrong with enjoying the fruits of our labor. God simply wants us to be wise as we manage our money so we can honor Him, live well and do good for others. Paul continued,

> *Tell them to use their money to do good. They should be rich in good works and generous to those in need, always being ready to share with others. By doing this they will be storing up their treasure as a good foundation for the future so that they may experience true life.* (1 Timothy 6:18–19)

Financial storms begin to whip up in our lives when we forget where our money comes from. When we think we are the sole source of the income passing through our bank accounts, we close our fists, claim ownership and get into trouble. Consider Jesus' words:

> *Don't store up treasures here on earth, where moths eat them and rust destroys them, and where thieves break in and steal. Store your treasures in heaven, where moths and rust cannot destroy, and thieves do not break in and steal.* ***Wherever your treasure is, there the desires of your heart will also be.*** (Matthew 6:19–21, emphasis added)

If we focus on accumulating wealth on this earth, we act like our primate friends—trading something of little value (treasures on earth) for something of eternal value (treasures in heaven). But when we open our hands and release our raging storms of financial stress to God, He will replace the space in our palms with unshakable financial peace. There is nothing more freeing.

DISCOVERING FINANCIAL PEACE

Financial peace is closely tied to God-honoring financial management, or stewardship. Unfortunately, stewardship has become a taboo topic. People in positions of Christian leadership are often afraid to broach the subject, which has left everyone else confused. But stewardship is part of life. We are stewards of our time, our abilities . . . and our money. We'll never be able to live the life God created us to live without first learning how to handle our resources the way God intends.

We'll never be able to live the life God created us to live without first learning how to handle our resources the way God intends.

Jesus was never afraid to talk about money. Outside of the kingdom of God, stewardship was His favorite subject. He talked more about money and possessions than about faith and prayer combined. There are over 2,350 verses in the Bible concerning money and how to deal with money. If I were asked to sum up all of His teachings on money and possessions in one sentence, it would be this: live an openhanded life. Closed-handed living is the quickest way to block God's blessing and miss out on privileges that can be considered life's true riches—riches such as being able to make a difference, investing in other people and leaving a legacy.

Living an openhanded life becomes much easier when you grasp the reality that God owns everything anyway. He is not only the source of your money and possessions; He is the owner. You are simply a manager of what He has allocated to you. When you absorb the magnitude of this truth and start to live accordingly, the financial storms around you will begin dying down.

Making the transition to openhanded living won't happen overnight, but there are four practical steps you can take to help you get there. The first step is to determine your financial priorities. Second, decide to get out of whatever debt you have accumulated. Third, discipline yourself in small financial ways. Finally, discover the incredible joy of generosity. As you are faithful to do these four things, God will honor your efforts at wise stewardship of His blessings. Let's look at each step in more detail.

Determine Your Priorities

Stewardship is ultimately about priorities. When it comes to time, relationships, talents and especially money, you manage what you have according to what you think is important. Take a look at the difference in how the two couples in the following scenarios manage their money:

Couple A—A couple in your neighborhood earns a combined income of $120,000 annually. Not too little by any means, but not extravagant either. But there's a problem: they are spending $130,000 per year.

Couple B—Another couple in your neighborhood also earns $120,000. This couple only spends $115,000 per year.

Couple B has much more financial peace than Couple A because they spend less money than they make. They fit their lifestyle into the parameters of their income.

Financial peace has little to do with how much money you earn and everything to do with how much you spend. In other words, financial peace has little to do with how much you make and everything to do with how you use what you make. You may be earning more money right now than you ever thought you would, yet you are still under crushing financial strain. As your income has increased, your peace has decreased. Why? Likely because you can relate too well to Couple A.

The difference between Couple A and Couple B is one word: priorities. Wise prioritizing is a significant stepping stone toward financial peace.

What are you putting first in your financial life? What are your priorities? Are they your wants and desires . . . or are they something else? Jesus said:

> *Seek first His kingdom and His righteousness, and all these things will be added to you.* (Matthew 6:33 NASB)

The Message translation (in more context) puts it this way:

> *If God gives such attention to the appearance of wildflowers—most of which are never even seen—don't you think he'll attend to you, take pride in you, do his best for you? What I'm trying to do here is to get you to relax, to not be so preoccupied with getting, so you can respond to God's giving. People who don't know God and the way he works fuss over these things,*

> *but you know both God and how he works. Steep your life in God-reality, God-initiative, God-provisions. Don't worry about missing out. You'll find all your everyday human concerns will be met.* (Matthew 6:30–33 MSG)

When your top priority is seeking God's best, everything else in your life will fall in line. Proper priorities lead to proper living; improper priorities lead to improper living.

> ***Financial peace has little to do with how much you make and everything to do with how you use what you make.***

The question then becomes, what does it look like to manage money in a way that gives God top priority? First of all, when money comes in, don't close your fist around it. Open your hand and thank God for the income. Then, tell that money where to go—if you don't, you'll end up wondering where it went. The first 10% of your gross income goes back to God as a tithe. We are commanded to return the first tenth of what God blesses us with back to him. As we do, He will continue to meet, and even exceed, our needs:

> *Honor the* L*ORD with your possessions,*
> *And* ***with the firstfruits of all your increase;***
> *So your barns will be filled with plenty,*
> *And your vats will overflow with new wine.*
> (Proverbs 3:9–10 NKJV, emphasis added)

Tithing is a big discussion that goes far beyond the scope of these pages. To dig deeper into what God has to say about tithing, see my book *The Generosity Ladder: Your Next Step to Financial Peace* (Baker Books).

After you give the first 10% of your income back to God, the second 10% goes to pay off debt. The third 10% goes into savings. If you are out of debt, congratulations! In your case, put the second 10% into savings and invest the third 10%. Use the other 70% of your income however you see fit. Learning to live on 70% of your earnings is essential to your long-term financial peace. Unfortunately, most people are living on 110%, spending everything they've got and then using credit to spend even more. That will land you smack in the middle of a financial storm every time.

You may be thinking, *I can't live on 70% now, but if I earned more money, then maybe I could.* That thought process is a trap. Studies have proven that when household incomes increase, lifestyles tend to increase accordingly. More money usually equals more stuff rather than more peace. You have to decide to end the cycle. With God's help, you can do it. You can free yourself of debt and start saving for your future. You can discover the peace and blessing that come with putting Him first in your finances and managing your money according to His principles.

THE 70% PRINCIPLE OF LASTING WEALTH

Learn to live on 70% of your income.

If you are in debt:

- First 10% to **tithe**.
- Second 10% to **debt**.
- Third 10% to **savings**.

If you are not in debt:

- First 10% to **tithe**.
- Second 10% to **savings.**
- Third 10% to **investments**.

For more detailed teaching on this principle or for more information on wise financial planning, see The Generosity Ladder: Your Next Step to Financial Peace *(Baker Books).*

Decide to Get Out of Debt

The average American carries over $17,000 of debt. Are you average? Above average? If you've ever been in a significant amount of debt, you understand the stress it brings. Millions in this country lie awake at night wondering how to pay off what they owe. As a culture, we have accepted the lie that credit and its accompanying debt is a necessary way of life, essential to maintaining the lifestyle we deserve.

God takes a different approach. He says someone who borrows money becomes a slave to the one who lends it (Proverbs 22:7). Have you ever felt like a slave to your credit card company or to a friend or family member who gave you a loan? God also calls those who borrow and don't repay wicked (Psalm 37:21). He says not to owe anyone anything other than your love (Romans 13:8).

Getting out of debt is possible. It's a process that begins with a decision. It is also one of the wisest steps you can take toward financial peace. Once you decide you don't want to live with the weight of debt dragging you down, you can begin the journey of becoming debt-free. Not only will your decision please God, but you'll also be putting yourself in a position where He is better able to bless you.

The first step to getting out of debt is to stop unnecessary spending. Refuse to dig any deeper into the hole you are standing in. Choose instead to embrace The Principle of Contentment—that is, be content with the things you already have instead of constantly longing for something newer, prettier, bigger or faster:

Don't love money; be satisfied with what you have. For God has said, "I will never fail you. I will never abandon you." (Hebrews 13:5)

When you embrace The Principle of Contentment, you don't feel the need to have the newest car or clothes. You don't have to run out and buy the latest iPhone; you can be happy with the one you are using—the one that was the latest and greatest six months or a year ago. You don't have to get those new boots you've had your eye on; you can squeeze one more season out of the ones you already have. You get the picture. You have to stop going further into debt before you can begin digging your way out.

Imagine how much extra money you would have if no credit card bills came in every month. Imagine being able to walk into a store and buy whatever you want with cash. Imagine the freedom of knowing you don't owe anyone money. Being debt-free brings incredible serenity. You can get there. Decide to stop the madness and adopt a smarter way of life. Your financial peace will multiply. To learn more about creating a plan for getting out of debt, see my book *The Generosity Secret: How to Get Out of Debt and Find Financial Freedom* (Baker Books) and visit www.BeUnshakable.com.

Discipline Yourself in Small Financial Ways

You've probably heard the saying, "The devil is in the details." Well, I like to spin that a bit. Actually, God is in the details. The Bible says that if we are faithful with the little things in life, we will be entrusted with more. How we deal with details matters, especially when it comes to money:

> *If you are faithful in little things, you will be faithful in large ones. But if you are dishonest in little things, you won't be honest with greater responsibilities. And if you are untrustworthy about worldly wealth, who will trust you with the true riches of heaven? And if you are not faithful with other people's things, why should you be trusted with things of your own? No one can serve two masters. . . . You cannot serve both God and money.* (Luke 16:10–13)

Over time, small, everyday decisions can majorly impact your financial life. By taking the initiative to examine your spending habits and figure out where your money is going, you can identify the areas that would most benefit from daily discipline. For example, not long ago, I started paying closer attention to my food costs. I was surprised by what I found. I had been in the habit of stepping out of the office for a sandwich or salad for lunch almost every day. Given my location, a typical lunch cost me anywhere from $11 to $15. When I started adding that cost up, I realized I was spending about $200 per month on lunch. That's over $2,600 every year—$8,000 over three years.

Seeing the actual price tag for my lunches made me realize I was throwing money away. Instead of continuing to go with the flow and watch my income disappear, I decided to start bringing my lunch to work. After all, I could make a sandwich at home for about $1. Once I understood what kind of money I could save by brown-bagging, my homemade sandwiches started tasting more delicious than anything I could buy in a restaurant. This simple discipline freed up money in my account that needed to be used for more important things.

What habits do you have that are slowly depleting your money? Do you spend $4 on a cup of coffee every day? That adds up to $124 every month—$1,460 per year. What could you do with that extra $1,460 if you started brewing your coffee at home? If you are in debt, you could start paying off what you owe. If you need to invest for the future, there's almost $1,500 you didn't have last year; you could add it to an existing money market account and start earning higher dividends. Or you could keep sweetening it with cream and sugar and drinking it down. Your small financial decisions—whether wise or otherwise—will slowly shape your financial future.

If you were to interview the wealthiest people in America, you may be surprised to find that they are the kind of people who eat humble lunches. They drink their own coffee. They drive slightly older cars. Studies show that the vast majority of wealthy people are not extravagant. Rather, they make small exchanges every day to ensure they stay on the path to wealth.

Unshakable Principle VII:

Turn Pain into Purpose

Your initial reaction may be to think of this kind of discipline as painful. In reality, it brings freedom from the stress of debt, the fear of not having enough and the storms of poor financial management. As you take steps toward discipline, keep the purpose behind what you are doing in mind, and the perceived pain will shift accordingly. Perhaps you've already experienced a financial crisis due to not living a disciplined life in the past. Don't let yourself forget that. In the spirit of Unshakable Principle VII, let that pain become your purpose for choosing discipline from here on out.

Disciplined spenders avoid the major financial storms that overtake those around them and relax instead in the calm breezes of financial peace. Be willing to discipline yourself in small ways, and you will put yourself in a position for God to bless you more than you can imagine:

> *So let's not get tired of doing what is good. At just the right time we will reap a harvest of blessing if we don't give up.* (Galatians 6:9)

Discover the Joy of Generosity

An inclination to give is written on your soul, no matter how diluted it may be. Sometimes, it takes a traumatic experience to bring that God-given pull toward generosity to the surface. Horror novelist Stephen King is not someone who is usually associated with biblical principles, but he understands this one. In a commencement speech delivered to Vassar graduates several years ago, he offered insight into living an open-handed life. Here's an excerpt of his comments:

> *A couple of years ago, I found out what "you can't take it with you" means. I found out while I was lying in a ditch at the side of a country road, covered with mud and blood and with the tibia of my right leg poking out the side of my jeans*

like a branch of a tree taken down in a thunderstorm. I had a MasterCard in my wallet, but when you're lying in a ditch with broken glass in your hair, no one accepts MasterCard.

We all know that life is ephemeral, but on that particular day and in the months that followed, I got a painful but extremely valuable look at life's simple backstage truths. We come in naked and broke. We may be dressed when we go out, but we're just as broke. Warren Buffet? Going to go out broke. Bill Gates? Going out broke. Tom Hanks? Going out broke. Steve King? Broke. Not a crying dime.

All the money you earn, all the stocks you buy, all the mutual funds you trade—all of that is mostly smoke and mirrors. It's still going to be a quarter-past getting late whether you tell the time on a Timex or a Rolex. No matter how large your bank account, no matter how many credit cards you have, sooner or later things will begin to go wrong with the only three things you have that you can really call your own: your body, your spirit and your mind.

So I want you to consider making your life one long gift to others. And why not? All you have is on loan, anyway. All that lasts is what you pass on. . . .

. . . We have the power to help, the power to change. And why should we refuse? Because we're going to take it with us? Please. Giving is a way of taking the focus off the money we make and putting it back where it belongs—on the lives we lead, the families we raise, the communities that nurture us.

A life of giving—not just money, but time and spirit—repays. It helps us remember that we may be going out broke, but right now we're doing O.K. Right now we have the power to do great good for others and for ourselves.

> *So I ask you to begin giving, and to continue as you began. I think you'll find in the end that you got far more than you ever had, and did more good than you ever dreamed.*[10]

Who knows how familiar Mr. King is with the Old Testament, but, intentionally or not, his remarks perfectly echoed the book of Ecclesiastes' observation:

> *We all come to the end of our lives as naked and empty-handed as on the day we were born. We can't take our riches with us.* (Ecclesiastes 5:15)

His words also spoke to the truth that takes the sting out of our condition:

> *It is more blessed to give than to receive.* (Acts 20:35)

Haven't you come to that conclusion in your own life? We all do at some point. Our perspective on giving and receiving eventually matures to embrace the truth. For example, when I was a kid, getting Christmas presents was the greatest thing in the world. I bet you felt the same way. But as I got older, my excitement over what I was going to get started being overtaken by my desire to give my parents and siblings something meaningful. Now that I have a wife and family of my own, I fully understand that true joy has nothing to do with getting gifts but with giving to the people I love. Haven't you felt that too? Coming to this realization is vital to living an openhanded life.

God is a giving God. He went so far as to give His own Son (John 3:16). So when you and I give, we are acting like Him.

No wonder there is so much power in generosity. As you begin to discover the joy of giving generously, you will step into a world of freedom and impact you never knew existed. See *The Generosity Secret: How to Get Out of Debt and Find Financial Freedom* (Baker Books) to dig deeper into the call to live a generous life.

Your dream for your financial future can become a reality. Begin by giving God top priority in your money, getting out of debt, disciplining yourself in small ways and dabbling in the joy of generosity. You don't have to be whipped around by the gale-force winds of a bad economy or a weak stock market. You can stand strong against financial stress and despair. Just open your hand and release the burden of your financial storms to God; He will be faithful to replace them with His peace.

CHAPTER 12

MARRIAGE ISSUES

Outfitting the Ultimate Marriage Survival Kit

A good marriage isn't something you find; it's something you make.

—Gary L. Thomas

So now I am giving you a new commandment: Love each other. Just as I have loved you, you should love each other.

—Jesus (John 13:34)

The sobering statistics about marriage are no secret. Half of the marriages in America ending in divorce has, sadly, become a cultural norm. Many people today think of the marital relationship as a temporary contract—something they get into with the best of intentions but know they can get out of if and when things get hard.

The very idea of marriage in our society is continually being questioned. Just consider the rampant public and political debate over the traditional, biblical understanding of marriage. Is marriage meant to be one man and one woman together forever? Or can it be something else? Differing perspectives and strong opinions abound.

Given the hostile climate toward marriage that permeates our culture, protecting our marriages is harder—and more important—than ever before. Our marriages are entangled in a war, just as many of us are at war within them. In any threatening situation like this, it helps to have a survival kit filled with the essential tools for standing strong and helping us return to the solid place of peace and love we inhabited when we first took our marriage vows. When we view marriage through the right lens and put some tools to work to protect our sacred union from the ravages of the world, we can have marriages that not only survive the dangerous storms whipping around them but also thrive in their midst.

SURVIVING AND THRIVING

God has a plan for your marriage. He wants it to be a strong, unshakable union of mutual love and respect. Just look at what Jesus said about marriage, as recorded by His disciple Matthew:

> *Some Pharisees came and tried to trap [Jesus] with this question: "Should a man be allowed to divorce his wife for just any reason?"*
>
> *"Haven't you read the Scriptures?" Jesus replied. "They record that from the beginning 'God made them male and female.' " And he said, "This explains why a man leaves his*

> *father and mother and is joined to his wife, and the two are united into one. Since they are no longer two but one, let no one split apart what God has joined together."* (Matthew 19:3–6)

God's plan for your marriage is that it will last forever and that it will be the most fulfilling human relationship in your life. You may be wondering if either of those things is even possible. They both are. Your marriage can survive—even thrive—but it takes work. You can't coast through your marriage and expect it to remain strong. You have to open your eyes to your responsibility to keep your relationship on course and healthy.

> ***God's plan for your marriage is that it will last forever and that it will be the most fulfilling human relationship in your life.***

When I stood before my family, friends and God at my wedding, I made some strong, specific commitments to my wife. But like most grooms, I didn't know what I was getting into. Besides love, I had no clue what it took to make a marriage work. I didn't have what I needed to survive . . . and neither did you on your wedding day. Thankfully, in navigating my own marriage and in working with hundreds of couples to strengthen theirs, I have been able to identify five tools (and their unique respective purposes) we all need to put in our storm survival kits to ensure that our marriages are still healthy and happy on our golden anniversaries.

THE MARRIAGE SURVIVAL KIT

Alarm Clock

Schedule Time for One Another

Modern Americans work an average of 11 hours more per week than Americans did 20 years ago. We are an achievement-crazed culture. Plus, on top of work, we have countless other obligations. Add in kids and all of their commitments, and we don't have a lot of free time to play with. Carving out time that's dedicated to your spouse can be tough, but making the effort is well worth it. The number one gift you can give your spouse is quality time.

If you've ever gardened, you may know that a rose bush can survive for a long time on just a little bit of water. But to make a rose bush bloom into the beauty God intends for it, you have to give it lots of water. Lack of water won't kill the bush; it will just keep it from flourishing. The same is true of time in your marriage. You may be able to get by without spending real quality time with your spouse for weeks, months or even years, but you will not have a flourishing relationship.

The first and best way to make quality time with your spouse a priority is to put it on your calendar, just as you would anything else important to you. Start by scheduling a weekly date night. Hire a babysitter and go out to dinner, or send the kids to a neighbor's house and cook dinner together. Take the time to reconnect. For my wife and me, every Thursday night is date night. We may both be barreling in different directions Monday through Wednesday, but we know that on Thursday night, we've set time aside for each other. I highly recommend making date night a regular part of your schedule.

Secondly, consider scheduling intimacy with your spouse. Yes, I mean schedule sex. You may push back a little on this idea, but stay with me. In our day, we have this idea that sex with our partner is supposed to happen spontaneously—that we are to be romantically swept into it every time, candles, rose petals and all. But in reality, things don't usually work out that way. Life gets busy. We are tired. The kids have a lot of homework. Your spouse gets called in to work. And suddenly, another week or month is gone and the two of you haven't shared any intimacy.

A popular article in the magazine *Marriage Partnership* talks about the idea of scheduling sex.[11] The article says that scheduling sex is important for many reasons. First of all, it eliminates the ask/beg factor. No explanation needed.

Secondly, instead of being unromantic, scheduled sex can feel just the opposite. Planning for it increases desire. You know it's going to happen later, so you think about it during the day. The anticipation builds. And you don't have to go through the whole "is it going to happen tonight/is it not going to happen tonight" dance. One note of caution the article gives is to make sure you put scheduled sex on your calendar in code. That will help you avoid some potentially embarrassing situations!

Planning also helps you give this intimate time with your spouse the attention it deserves. When we let sex fall into the crevices of life, it doesn't get our highest focus. We may be run down or distracted. We may have forgotten to shave. When you plan in advance, you can be ready to give the best of yourself to your mate. So, while scheduling sex may sound rigid at first, it has a lot of benefits. When you use this technique well, it just makes things in the bedroom better. Neglecting this important part of your marriage, on the other hand, can lead to a multitude of problems. For more tips and teaching on enhancing romance in your marriage, go to www.BeUnshakable.com.

Rose-Colored Glasses

See the Best in One Another

You've probably heard how important it is to accept your spouse "warts and all." That may sound like silly advice, but it is entirely biblical. You are called to love your spouse despite his or her imperfections. In a letter to believers in Ephesus, Paul wrote:

> *Always be humble and gentle. Be patient with each other, making allowance for each other's faults because of your love.* (Ephesians 4:2)

Paul's words are pertinent to every relationship we have in life. To foster the most successful marriage possible, though, we must take it a step beyond simply overlooking each other's faults. In marriage, there are three levels of love:

- **Love Level One:** I want to change my spouse and eradicate their faults. This is immature love.

- **Love Level Two:** I will look past my spouse's faults and love them even though they're not perfect. This is good, as noted, but it's not the highest level of love.
- **Love Level Three:** I will always try to see my spouse in the best possible light. I will look for the positive rather than the negative. This is an expression of the highest level of love in marriage.

A recent study from The State University of New York in Buffalo backs up the fact that Love Level Three leads to better marriages. SUNY researchers studied the marriages of couples who rated themselves as happy after many years together. They found that the most successful and happiest marriages are those in which each spouse has a higher opinion of their mate than the mate has of themselves. In short, they concluded that the most important quality of a successful marriage is the ability of each spouse to focus on the good in the other.

Oscar Wilde once said, "Marriage is the triumph of imagination over intelligence." Maybe he was getting at this principle. Seeing the good in your mate comes naturally when you are in the throes of infatuation and early love. But as marriage breeds familiarity between you, keeping that same perspective is largely a choice. Every human being is a combination of positive and negative attributes. When it comes to your spouse, you get to choose which attributes to focus on. Here's a little tip: the attributes you focus on are generally the ones that will rise to the top.

When Kelley and I were on our honeymoon—the day after we were married, actually—we got into a little fender bender. I thought it was the other driver's fault; he thought it was mine. When the police officer arrived, he saw things my way, which made the other guy furious. In his anger, this guy turned to Kelley and said, "You just married this man, right?" She said, "Yes." Then he pointed at me and said, "How does it feel to have just married a liar?" At that, Kelley jumped up, put her finger in the guy's face and said, "My husband is not a liar! He's the most honest person I have ever met, and you better not say that again!" She was on fire. The police officer actually had to ask me to "take my wife back to the car and leave."

Kelley was wearing rose-colored glasses that day. I'm not the most honest person in the world, but knowing she saw me that way made me want to be more truthful. As Goethe once said, "The way you see people is the way you treat them, and the way you treat them is what they become." You can positively shape your spouse's behavior by looking for the best in her and treating her accordingly. Find the beauty in your spouse even when she doesn't see it in herself. And wives, vice versa.

Song of Songs is the Bible's most romantic book. In essence, it is a love letter between two young lovers. The letter recounts the lovers' views of one another in this way:

Young Man

Like a lily among thistles
is my darling among young women.

Young Woman

Like the finest apple tree in the orchard
is my lover among other young men.
(Song of Songs 2:2–3)

As these two young lovers did, choose to see your spouse as head and shoulders above everyone else.

White Flag

Surrender the Fight to be Right

No marriage can exist in perpetual harmony. There will be misunderstandings and conflict. That's okay. When two people agree on everything, one of them isn't necessary. As Alan Patrick Herbert said, "The conception of two people living together for 25 years without having a cross word suggests a lack of spirit only to be admired in sheep." Since arguments are inevitable, the key is to learn when it's okay to argue and when it's not.

Kelley and I tend to argue over the smallest things. Can you relate? Most of our fights aren't over big decisions or future hopes and dreams but over mundane nothingness. Over the years, I've learned that when it comes to arguing over the small stuff, you have a choice: you can choose to be right, or you can choose to be happy. Consider what Paul's mentee, Timothy, wrote:

> *Remind everyone about these things, and command them in God's presence to stop fighting over words. Such arguments are useless, and they can ruin those who hear them. . . . Again*

> *I say, don't get involved in foolish, ignorant arguments that only start fights.* (2 Timothy 2:14, 23)

I don't know about you, but I need to write those verses down and keep them where I can see them every day.

Humility is the underlying issue when surrendering your right to be right. When you are humble, you don't feel the need to be right all the time. You don't have to win every battle. You can admit when you are wrong. Next time you feel your temper rising over something relatively insignificant, pause and ask yourself if that thing is worth ruining your day over. If not, be humble enough to be the one to bow out of the scuffle. Surrender your right to prove that you are right. Being able to do that makes you the winner.

In the greatest chapter on love in the entire Bible, the apostle Paul wrote:

> *Love is patient and kind. Love is not jealous or boastful or proud or rude. It does not demand its own way. It is not irritable, and it keeps no record of being wronged. It does not rejoice about injustice but rejoices whenever the truth wins out. Love never gives up, never loses faith, is always hopeful, and endures through every circumstance.* (1 Corinthians 13:4–7)

Those are wise words for us to live by in our love relationships. If we can learn to give away love that is patient and kind, not jealous, proud, boastful, rude or irritable; if we can love in a way that causes us to never keep a record of wrongs (that's a big one, isn't it?); if we can learn to walk in love that never loses faith and is always hopeful; if we can learn to live a love that endures through every circumstance, then we will have cultivated a love that will allow our marriages to thrive at the highest level.

Bottle of Repellant

Shut the Door on Temptation

Like pesky ants or cockroaches scurrying in a storm, temptation comes at us from every corner. It is always lurking in the shadows, just waiting for the right time to make itself known. Our culture is filled with temptation—eat this, buy that, look at her, sleep with him. In the war against your marriage, one of your best offensive moves is to be intentional about shutting the door on sexual temptation. Repel it before it has the chance to infest your relationship.

The enemy would love nothing more than to destroy the union you entered into before God. So he is constantly sending temptation your way. Any of us can be tempted; none of us is immune.

When I first married, I thought that was the end of temptation. After all, I had found the woman I wanted to spend the rest of my life with. I loved her more than words; she was the most beautiful creature I'd ever seen. However, I quickly learned that temptation doesn't leave you alone just because you put a wedding band on your finger. Sometimes, as is Satan's plan, taking a step of commitment makes temptation even worse. Don't let it surprise you. Since we are all tempted, and that's not likely to change on this earth, we have to learn how to handle temptation.

The Bible tells us that sin crouches at the door of every marriage; it is hanging out in the shadows, ready and willing to take you down at any moment. If you think you are immune to temptation, consider Paul's warning:

> *If you think you are standing strong, be careful not to fall. The temptations in your life are no different from what others experience.* (1 Corinthians 10:12–13)

No one stands at the altar and plans to have an affair or to become addicted to internet pornography, yet these things happen every day. Why? Because people don't plan not to. They play with fire and end up getting burned. They make a series of small decisions that ultimately lead to a catastrophe. They tiptoe too close to the edge of morality, and then, with the slightest push, they fall off the cliff.

So what's the answer? How do you shut the door on sexual temptation and protect your marriage?

> *Run from sexual sin! No other sin so clearly affects the body as this one does. For sexual immorality is a sin against your own body.* (1 Corinthians 6:18)

Do as Paul said and run! Run away! When you see sexual temptation in the distance, run! It's no coincidence that Paul repeated this in several places (again in 2 Timothy 2:22) just to drive home the point. Do whatever you have to do to get away from temptation.

There's nothing more important than your marriage and your family. So if there's someone at work who is causing you to lust, run. If someone in your neighborhood is tempting you, run. If someone at your gym piques your interest sexually, find a new gym. Do not play with sexual temptation. You have a responsibility to do everything in your power to protect your marriage and your spouse at all costs. Guarding your life against sexual temptation will go a long way toward ensuring that you don't end up as another infidelity statistic. I know some of you may be thinking, *Oh, but you don't know me. That will never happen to me.* It can happen to you as easily as it can happen to anyone else. Take a look at *The Message* translation of the Scripture from 1 Corinthians already noted:

> *Don't be so naive and self-confident. You're not exempt. You could fall flat on your face as easily as anyone else.* (1 Corinthians 10:12)

The more confident you are that you will never fall into sexual temptation, the harder Satan will work to make you fall. Don't let that happen. At the first sign of temptation, run!

Practically speaking, this means you don't talk to a person of the opposite sex about your problems or your personal life. It means you don't take a second look when you pass an attractive person on the street. It means you block sexually oriented sites on your computer or phone if you need to, or get an accountability partner to help you stay away from them. You've got to draw a hard line in the sand and say, "I am choosing to build a wall of protection around myself and my spouse. I am repelling sexual temptation. I am closing the door on potential dangers to my marriage."

So many people who fall into sexual temptation default to the excuses "I didn't mean to" or "I didn't have a choice."

Infidelity doesn't just happen. Sexual addictions don't just happen. You have a choice *every day* to live in a way that protects your marriage. Run! If you are struggling with temptation, turn to Chapter 6, which goes into more detail about how to stand strong against it.

What happens if you've already faced infidelity in your marriage? Maybe you are dealing with your spouse's or your own infidelity right now. Deciding how to handle the aftermath if one of you does fall into temptation is also an important discussion. In the Bible, Jesus said that infidelity is grounds for divorce, but He never said you *should* divorce because of infidelity. As hurtful as this situation can be, you don't have to give up on your marriage.

> ***Infidelity doesn't just happen. Sexual addictions don't just happen. You have a choice every day to live in a way that protects your marriage.***

A recent study shows that two-thirds of married couples who decide to stay together and try to make it through infidelity are happy after five years.[12] Why should you try to stay together at all costs? Because your marriage is sacred to God. He wants to protect your marriage, and a mistake on your part doesn't change that. He doesn't throw His hands up and say, "Well, that one's over!" No, He still sees your marriage as holy and wants to heal it.

If the offending spouse is willing to ask for forgiveness, change his or her ways and recommit to the relationship, you have to ask yourself if you can, with God's strength, accept that. If the answer is yes, do the hard work of putting things back together. But even more importantly, shut the door on temptation on the front end and spare you and your spouse the harm and pain that infidelity causes.

Compass and Map

Set the Spiritual Direction for Your Marriage

When you get married, something becomes the master of your relationship. That something is different for every couple. Perhaps you each serve yourselves and see marriage as an arrangement where your spouse's job is to make you happy. Maybe you and your spouse have decided to serve money, your careers or your family. Whatever it is, you are serving *something*. If you want your marriage to go beyond surviving to thriving, you and your spouse must choose to serve God. Setting the spiritual direction of your marriage toward God is one of the most important marital decisions you can make.

What does serving God together look like? At its base level, you each have to decide individually to make God and His Son, Jesus, your foundation. Then, as a couple, you move in His direction together by:

- **Praying Together:** Praying together is truly one of the secrets to a strong marriage. Like the old cliché says, "Couples who pray together stay together!" As cheesy as it may sound, it became a cliché because statistics prove it to be overwhelmingly true. You don't have to pray long, drawn-out prayers where you say all the names of God in Hebrew. Just say a simple prayer in the morning or before you go to bed at night. Reach over, grab your spouse's hand and ask God to bless your marriage. Have you ever asked Him to do that?

- **Reading the Bible Together:** It's important that you read the Bible on your own, but it's also important to incorporate it into the fabric of your marriage. When you need wisdom on a difficult situation—whether it's dealing with money wisely, handling a tough relationship or coping with an illness—go to the Bible together and search out the answer. Doing devotional studies together, or at least at the same time, is also great. You'll be able to talk with each other about what you are learning. For some Bible study suggestions, go to www.BeUnshakable.com.

- **Going to Church Together:** Make it a priority to be in church together regularly. You'll learn more about the Bible and draw closer to God, plus you'll have the chance to worship with other like-minded people.

- **Being in a Small Group Together:** One of the best ways you can commit to pointing your marriage in the right direction is by being around other couples doing the same. Find a biblically grounded small group of couples through your local church and take the sometimes scary step of joining. You will make new friends, grow in your faith and strengthen your marriage simultaneously.

Take a look at this triangle:

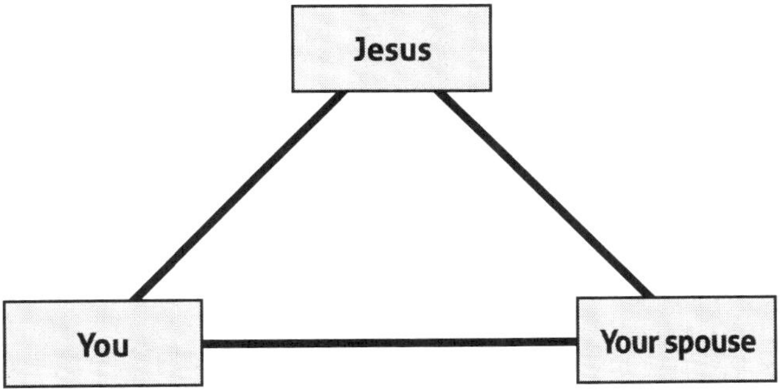

The key to having a solid marriage is to recognize that you and your spouse are not the only ones involved—Jesus is part of your marriage too. He has sanctified marriage as holy. Think of your marriage in terms of the triangle pictured here. The closer you and your spouse move toward Jesus individually, the closer you move toward each other. The further away you slide from Him, the further you slide from each other.

How does this work? Well, the more you become like Jesus, the more you're going to treat your spouse the way Jesus wants you to treat her. The more deeply you fall in love with Jesus and receive love from Him, the more love you'll have to give to your spouse. If both of you are becoming more like Christ, your marriage is going to get stronger. You will become closer to God and your spouse.

Note one more thing about the geometry of the triangle: if one of you is moving toward God while the other is moving away, you will be as far apart as you can get. Set your spiritual direction toward the triangle's peak and then move that way, individually and as a couple.

STORMS WILL COME

From triangles back to rose bushes . . . marriages are a lot like the roses I mentioned earlier. They are beautiful gifts from God, but they come with a few thorns, as all human relationships do. Every married couple can find a reason to call the whole thing off. Even marriages that are a week old can find grounds for divorce. The key is to continue finding reasons to stay together. Again, sidestep surprise. Don't be taken aback when the storms roll in, because they will.

More marriages would survive if the partners realized that the best times often come after the worst. Struggles make us stronger, individually and as a unit. So decide now that you aren't going to let tough times make you want to jump ship. No matter how things might feel during the storm, God wants to bless your marriage. God's blessing comes to those who persevere.

Marriage allows you to grow into the person God wants you to be in partnership with the person you love. When you apply God's plan to your marriage, you will find that marriage is a joy, full of hope and bright futures. But you have to choose to love. That's right, love is a choice. Just as God chose to love you, you can choose daily to love your spouse in the same way. When you do, your marriage will be better than you could have ever imagined.

CHAPTER 13

DISCONNECTION FROM GOD

Experiencing God's Presence Through Worship

An authentic life is the most personal form of worship. Everyday life has become my prayer.

—Sarah Ban Breathnach

Take your everyday, ordinary life—your sleeping, eating, going-to-work, and walking-around life—and place it before God as an offering. . . . Don't become so well-adjusted to your culture that you fit into it without even thinking. Instead, fix your attention on God. You'll be changed from the inside out.

—Paul (Romans 12:1–2 MSG)

Have you ever left a church service or a Bible study feeling like you just didn't get anything out of it? Have you been frustrated because you can't seem to connect with God when you want to, the way you want to? Maybe you've felt as if your prayers aren't making it any higher than the ceiling, or you've been wondering why the passion you once had for your relationship with God has dimmed, why all of your attempts to engage with Him in worship feel empty and wrong.

So much of the disconnection you and I feel from God at certain points in our spiritual walk is the result of misinformation about how we should be connecting with Him in the first place. We have accepted some false beliefs about what it means to come to God in reverence—that is, to worship Him. These false beliefs can keep us feeling tossed around by the perceived storms of God's silence and distance when, if we could just grasp the truth, we could stand firm and confident in our connection with Him. Here are the most common misconceptions we cart around:

Four Worship Myths

1. Worship is about me.
2. Worship is what happens in the hour I'm at church.
3. Worship is just a part of my life.
4. Worship is a religious act.

These four misconceptions have become so ingrained in the psyche of today's church that I call them myths. They have moved past being misinformation and have taken hold as false truth. They lead to an incorrect understanding that worship is about you, your preferences, what you feel, what you experience and what you can get. Such wrong thinking leads to a feeling of being shut out by God when the reality is that He's standing ready and waiting. Let's take a look at each of these four myths and the corresponding truths that debunk them:

Myth—*Worship is for you.*
Truth—*Worship is not for you but for God.*

Worship is not about you. The danger of making worship about your own feelings and desires is that, by doing so, you make yourself the focus. Even though you may be professing to worship God, you end up worshipping your own interests. No wonder this kind of worship leads to emptiness.

You and I were created and exist to bring pleasure to God. In fact, that's the definition of worship. As the New Testament says:

> *You are worthy, O Lord our God, to receive glory and honor and power. For you created all things, and they exist because you created what you pleased.* (Revelation 4:11)

When we make worship about ourselves, we fall into the trap of judging our worship based on our feelings. We rely on our emotions to tell us when we have connected with God. But worship is not always a warm and fuzzy feeling. Of course, God wants us to sense His presence, but He is much more concerned that we know Him in truth than that we feel Him. He is pleased by faith, not feelings.

In fact, I would argue that our worship should be even more treasured when we don't feel it. In those times, we know we have worshiped God because He is worthy, rather than out of a self-seeking heart. As A. W. Tozer wrote in his great work *The Purpose of Man*:

> *Worship is not confined to emotion and feelings, but is an inward attitude and a state of mind subject to degrees of perfection and intensity. It is not possible to always worship with the same degree of wonder and love as at other times, but wonder and love always has to be there.*[13]

As a pastor, I can't tell you how many times I've seen people come to church looking for something for themselves, only to leave feeling empty because they didn't receive what they thought they needed. Why? They were inwardly focused. If you approach worship with an attitude of "God, what do You have for me," you're always going to walk away empty. Instead, shift your perspective into alignment with God's truth by asking, "God, how can I give myself to You? How can I give You praise? How can I give You glory? How can I give You the worth You deserve?" Only then will you walk away from your time of worship deeply satisfied.

When you internalize the reality that worship is about offering your attention, your energy, your talent and your focus to God—that it's about giving Him the praise and adoration He deserves—you will begin to see your Father for who He is and begin to be able to worship Him in truth.

Myth— *Worship happens one day a week.*
Truth— *Worship is not just for Sunday, but every day.*

The early church understood that worship was an everyday activity. King David famously said:

> *I will praise the* L*ORD* *at* **all times**.
> *I will* **constantly** *speak his praises.*
> (Psalm 34:1, emphasis added)

Part of the reason we have moved away from constant worship and praise in today's culture is that we have turned church into something we go to and the idea of worship into something that happens at church. As such, we have begun perpetuating the idea that God lives in the church building and that we only worship Him on Sundays—if the worship songs tickle our fancy. Harsh? Maybe, but all too true.

This mindset is exacerbated by the fact that we live in a spectator society. We go to movies, plays and baseball games. We sit in front of our television sets, expecting to be entertained. This modern expectation has crept into the church as well; we take a seat and wait for the show to begin. But, as author Louie Giglio wrote in his work on praise and worship, *The Air I Breathe*, "Worship isn't something you attend, like a movie or a concert. Worship is something you enter into with all your might. Worship is a participation sport in a spectator culture."[14]

Contrary to popular belief, worship is not just something that takes place in a church service. In fact, it has little to do with actual planned services. While our participation on Sunday mornings is a requirement of a thriving faith, worship neither begins nor ends at church. Rather, worship is an activity God calls you and me to engage in each and every day—when we wake up in the mornings, when we hear our children laugh, when we feel overwhelmed at work, when we embrace our spouse, when we see a sunset, when money is tight, when we enjoy a great meal, when we see a long-lost friend, when our family members are driving us crazy, when we breathe in the spring breeze . . . you get the picture. Worship is an all-the-time, consistent endeavor, just as David modeled.

But since worship is not always going to be our default state of being—especially when things in life aren't going as well as we would like them to—we need to develop a worship habit to help us worship regularly and raise our level of continuous praise. Let me suggest an exercise: take the next 10 days and intentionally practice worshipping. Here are three simple steps to help you work a worship habit into your daily life:

1. *Give God Your First 15*: Commit to spending the first 15 minutes of your day with God. As soon as you roll out of bed, open your Bible and read a few passages. Spend a few minutes in prayer. If you don't know what to read, start with Psalms. It's full of ideas about how you can live a life of worship every day. For a detailed Bible reading plan, go to www.BeUnshakable.com.

2. *Say Breath Prayers*: Throughout your day, pray quick breath prayers. They may be something as simple as, "God, thank You for my job" or "God, help me deal with this situation with my children." Frequent, simple prayers remind you to both trust God and thank Him for what He is doing in your life.

3. *Pray at Bedtime*: Whether you said bedtime prayers as a child or not, it's time to pick up the practice. Before you go to sleep, take a few minutes to reflect on your day and acknowledge the ways God has blessed you. Thank Him for those blessings. Even if you had a difficult day, learning how to acknowledge God's continual presence and thank Him in every situation is key to living a life of worship. Situations change for better or for worse, but God's worth never changes.

Consider what the apostle Paul wrote in his letter to the Romans:

> *So here's what I want you to do, God helping you: Take your everyday, ordinary life—your sleeping, eating, going-to-work, and walking-around life—and place it before God as an offering. Embracing what God does for you is the best thing you can do for him. Don't become so well-adjusted to your culture that you fit into it without even thinking. Instead, fix your attention on God. You'll be changed from the inside out.* (Romans 12:1–2 MSG)

Paul's words provide the secret to living a life of worship every day. When you and I take our "everyday, ordinary life" and lay the details of it before God, we will move from being once-a-week worshipers to being daily worshipers. And, as Paul said, we will be changed from the inside out.

Myth— *Worship is just a part of your life.*
Truth— *Worship is not part of life, but all of life.*

Authentic worship—the kind of worship that isn't focused on you and doesn't just happen at certain times—is the natural response to a proper understanding of God. In its truest form, worship is the offering of your entire life up to God. It's a moment-by-moment, day-by-day activity that encompasses who you are. It's a way of life.

In fact, worship that is anything other than a lifestyle is something of a new invention. In biblical times, people were great at praising God continually. They praised Him at home, in battle, at parties and even in jail. Worship infused every area of life, which is God's plan and desire. Without a consistent lifestyle of worship, you will end up yo-yoing back and forth in frustrated pursuit of the peace and the potential God has already planned for you.

Real worship is all about falling in love with God; it's about entering into a relationship where you can't get enough of Him. You think of Him constantly and want to do the things that bring Him pleasure simply because you love Him. You want to give Him all of your life, everything about yourself.

Unfortunately, feelings like these don't always come naturally. They have to be encouraged and nourished. In fact, the Bible says that we need to be reminded to turn our thoughts to God every hour because if we don't, our mind begins to wander. Take a look at the psalmist's words:

> *From the rising of the sun to its setting,*
> *The name of the Lord is to be praised.* (Psalm 113:3 NASB)

When you read this verse, think of a sundial. As the sun moves across the sky, every single hour, the name of the Lord is to be praised.

I have to admit, I am often amazed by how long I can go without my thoughts turning to God. I am the pastor of a church with lots of locations and am engaged in training other pastors every day—in short, my entire life is focused on ministry—and yet, sometimes, I will go for hours without thinking about God. In the middle of the day, I'll realize I haven't acknowledged God since that morning. I have learned that I need daily reminders, even hourly reminders, to turn my attention back to God.

Again, choosing to start your day with praise is a great way to make sure you set out centered. Remembering to say those breath prayers throughout the day is a powerful reminder of your dependence on your Creator. Here's another idea that lots of people I've talked with have found helpful as a way to keep their conversation with God going all day: when you say your prayers in the morning, don't say *amen.* Don't put that finality on them. Just finish your prayer time with God and begin your day without signing off. Then, in a sense, everything you do during the day continues your time with Him. Of course, this is always the reality, but not saying *amen* will help keep you in the right mindset. You'll also be more likely to pick the conversation back up as your day unfolds.

I've also known people who like to give themselves an hourly reminder to turn their attention to God by setting an alarm. If they work at a desk, they may set an alarm on their computer to remind them to come before God for a few minutes. They may set a reminder on their watch or phone. Whatever the method, the whole point is to put a tool in place that will help them remember to turn their thoughts to God, from the rising of the sun to the setting of the same. Such simple reminders can help you and me enter into continual conversation and fellowship with the Creator as part of a lifestyle of worship.

When you begin making worship your lifestyle, you will sense God's peace and joy throughout the day. Not only will that allow you to face whatever comes your way with more assurance, but it will also reflect the beauty of constant communion with God to those around you. As you start being intentional about worship, remember Principle VI of Unshakable Faith: *Be a Willing Witness.* When others see the effects of your love for God manifesting through your everyday activities, don't be hesitant to tell them about His goodness.

Unshakable Principle VI:

Be a Willing Witness

Myth—*Worship is a religious activity.*
Truth—*Worship is not about a religion but a relationship.*

This may surprise you, but Christianity is not a religion. At its core, religion is about work—work for justification, favor, a better life, blessing and so on. However, neither Christianity nor worship has anything to do with this type of work. Religion is man-centered; Christianity is relationship-centered. Rather than being about what we do to earn God's favor, it's about who we are in Jesus Christ.

Digesting the reality that Christianity isn't a religion has the power to move us from what I call religious worship to authentic worship. Religious worship stifles authentic worship. Since religion focuses on acts, religious worship presses worshippers into a perversion of the type of worship that God intends. Worship becomes a game of "What can I do to get God to bless me?" We begin to think that if we sing the right way, repeat the Apostles' Creed or take Communion every week, God will respond by giving us what we need.

Don't misunderstand me: there's nothing wrong with wanting to sing well for God, repeating the Apostles' Creed or taking Communion regularly when it's done with the right motivation. But when these things—or anything for that matter—become religious rituals that you and I perform to win God's favor, we will miss authentic worship every time. God detests religious worship. Take a look at what He has to say about it in Isaiah:

> *And so the Lord says,*
> *"These people say they are mine.*
> *They honor me with their lips,*
> *but their hearts are far from me.*
> *And their worship of me*
> *is nothing but man-made rules learned by rote."*
> (Isaiah 29:13)

How is it that we are so easily persuaded into this kind of religious worship? Our Western culture is one of the culprits. We have been raised with a do-it-yourself mentality. As self-sufficient Westerners, we think in terms of cause and effect—what I do determines what I get. If we don't have what we need, we're told to pull ourselves up by our bootstraps and go after it harder. We think that if we control the variables, we control the outcome. While this may be a great attitude to have in many other areas of life, it is not true with God.

Being in a relationship with Jesus puts you in right standing with God—there's no other action you need to take to ensure His approval and your salvation—but that doesn't mean you stop taking the right actions. Rather, your motivation changes. You and I instinctively understand the underlying truth here regarding our human relationships. In a healthy relationship, we treat the other person with respect; we do things to please, rather than hurt or offend, our counterpart. We aren't trying to win approval anymore; we are simply acting out of the overflow of a good relationship. Right actions are the natural result of a right relationship. A heart to please is a byproduct of a loving, in-tune bond.

Here's the tricky part: right actions, on their own, do not necessarily indicate or guarantee a right relationship. It's possible to do all the right things for all the wrong reasons, as we've seen with religion. Religious thinking purports that if you do things the proper way, a relationship will follow. But, as I'm sure you are beginning to realize, this reasoning is backward. Instead, a right relationship should motivate you to do the right things out of love, not obligation. True worship, at its core, is the result of your heartfelt response to God's goodness and love.

AN AUDIENCE OF ONE

Connecting authentically with God comes as you offer your entire self and everything you do to Him as an act of worship every day. You don't live to please yourself or other people; you live to please your Father in heaven. You don't live to get what you can out of life; you live to give all you can to God . . . and let Him use you accordingly. In short, living a life of worship means living a life centered on pleasing an Audience of One—the One who created you, takes pleasure in you and wants to stay continually connected in a close relationship with you.

CHAPTER 14

DEATH

Facing the Death of People You Love with Strength

For death begins with life's first breath, and life begins at touch of death.

—John Oxenham

O death, where is your victory?
O death, where is your sting?

—Paul (1 Corinthians 15:55)

Some of the great comedians of our time have worked to bring a little humor to the complex subject of death. As George Carlin once put it, "Death is caused by swallowing small amounts of saliva over long periods of time." True enough. Woody Allen famously said, "I'm not afraid to die; I just don't want to be there when it happens." Have you ever felt that way? We all know death is inevitable; we just don't want to be there when it becomes official. Unfortunately, sidestepping mortality isn't an option. We have to deal with it throughout our lives. Loved ones will die. Friends will die. We will die. Death is an inevitable part of life's journey.

Think back to the first time death became a reality for you. I bet you can remember a specific moment. I can; I was six years old. One morning, my parents received a phone call that my grandmother had suffered a massive heart attack in her sleep. Even though I was only six, I knew something was wrong. I watched my frantic parents rush around the house, trying to get ready and get out the door. They dropped me off to spend the day with some relatives rather than taking me into the situation at my grandmother's house. I didn't even go to the funeral. But I knew something had changed in my world. Suddenly, death wasn't just for cartoon characters anymore.

As the years went by, I dealt with other losses. I had a cousin who died not long after my grandmother. In high school, a friend of mine committed suicide. About a decade into our marriage, Kelley and I faced a different sort of death: our pet bulldog, who had been with us for ten years, died of a brain tumor. More recently, both of my parents passed away. As anyone who has lost a parent knows, it's one of the most challenging and shaping things we walk through on this earth.

Do my experiences bring up any memories for you? Whose death have you had to deal with?

Death is extremely difficult, but it is a reality. Everything that lives eventually dies. When someone we love dies, we find ourselves caught in the throes of one of the worst storms life can bring our way. Learning to face death with faith is essential to making it to the other side of the pain. God knows that dealing with death is hard for us, so the Bible offers guidance.

In his letter to the church in Thessalonica, Paul addressed a group of Christians who had just lost someone close to them. Trying to help with their grieving, he wrote:

> *And now, dear brothers and sisters, we want you to know what will happen to the believers who have died so you will not grieve like people who have no hope.* (1 Thessalonians 4:13)

Paul was not supposing that people of faith would not grieve the death of their loved ones, just that we would not grieve like those "who have no hope." Grief and mourning are natural and necessary when we lose someone we love. He was not trying to sugarcoat the pain. Rather, he was highlighting the chasm between two different levels of understanding.

For the person whose life is built on a solid foundation of faith, death is tremendously heartbreaking but not unbearable because we have hope in heaven and the assurance that God has a plan. For the unbeliever, however, death is accompanied by unimaginable, inordinate sorrow because it truly is a final, bitter goodbye. Take a fresh look at Jesus' illustration concerning these two types of people:

> *Anyone who listens to my teaching and follows it is wise, like a person who builds a house on solid rock. Though the rain comes in torrents and the floodwaters rise and the winds beat against that house, it won't collapse because it is built on bedrock. But anyone who hears my teaching and doesn't obey it is foolish, like a person who builds a house on sand. When the*

> *rains and floods come and the winds beat against that house, it will collapse with a mighty crash.* (Matthew 7:24–27)

When your faith is built on bedrock, you can face the worst storms of life—even the death of someone you love—without being fundamentally shaken. But if you are building on a foundation of sand, you will not be able to stand. When death comes into your world, you will be like the hopeless mourners Paul referred to above. Later, in a letter to the Corinthian church, Paul wrote:

> *For we know that when this earthly tent we live in is taken down (that is, when we die and leave this earthly body), we will have a house in heaven, an eternal body made for us by God himself and not by human hands.* (2 Corinthians 5:1)

Death is always going to be one of the most painful things you and I have to face on this earth. But if we anchor our lives on faith in God and let what the Bible teaches about death become part of our understanding, we can find peace even in this most difficult situation.

FACING DEATH WITH FAITH

When death comes, there are several practical steps we can take to make sure we deal with the loss from a position of unshakable faith.

Turn Immediately to God

In the New Testament, Jesus' brother James teaches,

> *Come close to God, and God will come close to you.* (James 4:8)

But it can often seem difficult to "come close to God," especially after a loved one has just died. James was simply saying that you and I can draw close to God by admitting our anger and sadness to Him while at the same time acknowledging our need for and dependence on Him. When we do that, He will be right there with us.

Charles Spurgeon was the pastor of London's Metropolitan Baptist Tabernacle in the 1800s. During that time, the Tabernacle was the largest church in the world. As Spurgeon was teaching a crowd of about 10,000 people one fall evening, someone yelled, "Fire!" Chaos broke out. In the mad rush to get out of the arena, hundreds of people were injured, and seven were killed. Those seven deaths haunted Spurgeon for the rest of his life, as is proven by some of his later writings. For years, he struggled to make sense of what had happened. He didn't know the seven victims personally, but their deaths weighed on his soul. Even though he wrestled with God in an attempt to understand, he chose to draw close to Him at the same time. In return, God drew close to Spurgeon.

As the popular prose reminds us:

> *God is too wise to be mistaken. And God is too good to be unkind. When you can't trace His hand, you can always trust His heart.*

If we try to trace the hand of God in the circumstances that led to the death of a loved one, we may be left distraught and carrying a load that God never intended for us to shoulder. But if we choose to draw close to Him, trusting His heart and acknowledging His goodness, He will draw close to us and become our source of comfort. We will experience God in an entirely new way.

King David faced some big losses in his life. During one particularly difficult season of loss, he wrote some verses you may be familiar with. Many people turn to this passage of Scripture when they are facing the death of someone they love. You and I should be quick to do the same:

The Lord is my shepherd;
I have all that I need.
He lets me rest in green meadows;
he leads me beside peaceful streams.
He renews my strength.
He guides me along right paths,
bringing honor to his name.
Even when I walk
through the darkest valley,
I will not be afraid,
for you are close beside me.
Your rod and your staff
protect and comfort me.
You prepare a feast for me
in the presence of my enemies.
You honor me by anointing my head with oil.
My cup overflows with blessings.
Surely your goodness and unfailing love will pursue me
all the days of my life,
and I will live in the house of the Lord
forever. (Psalm 23)

When you walk through death's shadow, God is walking with you. He's not sitting in heaven, saying, "Oh, I hope they get through this okay." No, He is there every step of the way to protect you and to give you comfort, assurance and strength. But first, you have to draw close to Him. Drawing close to God does not mean the pain will go away immediately, but God will begin to lead you through healing.

Give Yourself Permission to Mourn

Mourning is a natural part of healing. Not only that, it's biblical. There is a time to laugh and a time to cry, a time to dance and a time to grieve (Ecclesiastes 3:4). When we lose a loved one, grief and mourning are inevitable, but always in light of the hope of our faith.

Everyone who faces the death of a loved one will go through similar stages. Author Elisabeth Kübler-Ross most popularly defined these stages in her work *On Death and Dying*.[15] Interestingly, the stages of grief, as Kübler-Ross describes them, closely mirror what the Bible says about how we move through the grieving process:

- *Denial*—When someone we love dies, our initial response is to deny it. We don't let ourselves acknowledge the loss. But we can only stay in denial for so long. When the truth finally becomes unavoidable, we move to the next phase.
- *Anger*—Anger is an easy default emotion when we lose a loved one. And, while it is understandable, we should be careful to guard against anger directed at God and

choose instead to draw close to Him. He's the only one who can bring us peace.

- *Bargaining*—In the bargaining stage, we are tempted to exchange our pain for any kind of temporary relief we can find. That's why so many people turn to substance abuse after a loss. As their drug of choice quells the pain, they find some escape—but only momentarily. The problem with this trade-off is that the pain always comes back worse than before . . . which leads to more bargaining, which leads to more pain, which leads to more bargaining. You get the picture.
- *Depression*—Those who are grieving usually feel depression taking its toll anywhere from a few weeks to a couple of months after the death, as they see life around them continuing to go on in the absence of their loved one. This is when the reality of life after loss starts to set in.
- *Acceptance*—Acceptance is the final stage of grieving. Acceptance doesn't mean we get over it. We never get over the loss of someone close to us; it just becomes part of the fabric of who we are. Acceptance means acknowledging that God is in control and trusting His heart.

Admit You Need Support from Others

One of the worst mistakes we can make is to try to face the days after a friend or family member's death alone. Grief often makes us feel like closing the door on the rest of the world and looking for respite inside ourselves. We have to resist the urge. God doesn't intend for us to go through life's difficulties in solitude. We are not wired for it. We need support from others.

Remember Principle V of Unshakable Faith: *Borrow from Others.* When things get hard, we must surround ourselves with people from whom we can borrow faith and strength. We need people to help us hold on—hold on to our hope, hold up our attitude and take hold of our emotions. That's part of the reason God gave us the church. The church is a spiritual family, linked together by a common Father, that celebrates with us in good times and helps us get through the difficult times. As Paul wrote:

Unshakable Principle V:

Borrow from Others

> *Share each other's burdens, and in this way obey the law of Christ.* (Galatians 6:2)

You and I need to be quick to allow others to share our burdens; it's the only way we'll make it to the other side of the storm whole.

Use the Opportunity to Grow and Share Your Faith

When a death occurs, faith inevitably enters the discussion. In my decades as a pastor, I have been at the bedside of many dying people. I can tell you that there is a tremendous difference between someone who dies without faith in Jesus Christ and someone who dies with faith. Seeing that divide has motivated me to use the opportunity that death brings to talk to people about the reality of eternity. Death gives us a chance to be a willing witness, as Principle VI of Unshakable Faith says we should be—it gives an opportunity to point people toward God and to remind them of the hope we have in Jesus.

> ***Unshakable Principle VI:***
> ***Be a Willing Witness***

When the apostle Paul was facing his death, he wrote these famous words:

> *For to me, to live is Christ and to die is gain.* (Philippians 1:21 NASB)

How could Paul possibly have said that to die would be gain? Because when a person who believes in Jesus as their Savior passes away, they do gain—they gain heaven, eternity and the presence of Jesus Himself. Christianity is not only the best way to live; it's also the best way to die. There really is victory beyond the grave. As Paul wrote:

> *"Death is swallowed up in victory.*
> *O death, where is your victory?*
> *O death, where is your sting?" . . .*
> *Thank God! He gives us victory over sin and death through our Lord Jesus Christ.* (1 Corinthians 15:54–55, 57)

If you have built your life on a solid foundation of faith, the death of friends and family members—while not easy, by any means—won't be able to knock you into despair, as it does those with no hope. The storm may rage, but it won't overtake you. Thanks to Jesus, the sting of death has been removed. You can remain unshaken in its presence.

For more resources on dealing with the death of a loved one, go to www.BeUnshakable.com.

EPILOGUE

BUILDING ON THE RIGHT FOUNDATION

I became a follower of Christ a little differently and a little later than most people might expect. I asked Jesus to come into my life right around my 18th birthday. Until that point, I had been consumed with other things. I started and sold a computer business while I was in high school. When I hit 17, I was working on an engineering degree at North Carolina State University while traveling and speaking at different conferences for young entrepreneurs.

At one of these conferences, I met a guy who had written a book I wanted to read, so I headed to a local bookstore to pick it up. While I was there, I noticed a book by Billy Graham called *Peace With God.* I bought Dr. Graham's book on a whim, thinking it was a history book about a guy I had heard a little about while growing up in North Carolina.

So, in October of 1989, I was reading through *Peace With God* and got to the page where Billy Graham offered an invitation of salvation to anyone who didn't know Jesus. My heart was convicted. I prayed the prayer that Dr. Graham had written out for me and then saw a toll-free number that he suggested I call. I went back to my little apartment in Raleigh and called the number. Yep, I'm that guy. The person on the other end of the line suggested I do a few things— read my Bible, pray, get involved in a good church and make my decision public through baptism.

After I gave my life to God, He put me on a new path. I ended up getting my bachelor's degree in religion and psychology at Gardner-Webb University and then a Master of Divinity at Duke University while pastoring a little church outside of Charlotte, North Carolina. Eventually, I moved to southern California to work with Rick Warren and the Purpose Driven Community. In 2000, my wife, Kelley, and I moved to Manhattan to start The Journey Church of the City. Then, in 2010, we moved to Boca Raton, Florida, to start The Journey Church - Boca Raton.

While the details of our stories are different, one thing is the same: God is calling you to make the same decision about His Son. If you have never asked Jesus to come into your life, let me encourage you to pray the prayer I prayed that fall day in North Carolina:

> *Dear God, I open my heart to You and invite You into my life. I confess that I am a sinner. I ask that You forgive me for all that I've done wrong. Thank You for sending Your Son, Jesus, who died for me and who gives me the opportunity to know You. I want to be Your follower. Thank You for accepting me. In Jesus' name, I pray. Amen.*

If you just prayed that prayer from your heart, you are now part of God's family. Congratulations! Welcome to the journey. From now on, your life will be built on the solid foundation of faith in Jesus. You can find materials to answer your questions and show you what to do next at www.BeUnshakable.com. You've just made the greatest decision of your life!

SCRIPTURE GUIDE

Where To Find Help When You Are...

Afraid:

Psalm 27:1, 5; 34:4; 56:1–13; 91:1–16; Isaiah 35:4; 41:10; John 14–27; Hebrews 13:6; 1 John 4:18

Angry:

Psalm 37:8; Proverbs 14:29; 15:1; Matthew 5:22–24; Romans 12:10–21; Ephesians 4:26, 31–32; James 1:19–20

Anxious/Worried:

Psalm 37:5; 46:1–11; 55:22; Proverbs 3:5–6; Matthew 6:25–34; Philippians 4:6–7; 1 Peter 5:7

Bitter/Resentful:

Matthew 6:14–15; Romans 12:14–15; 1 Peter 2:23

Depressed:

Psalm 27:13–14; 34:1–22; 42:1–11; Isaiah 41:10; Matthew 11:28–30; Romans 8:28; Philippians 4:13

Discouraged/Disappointed:

Matthew 11:28–30; Romans 8:28; 2 Corinthians 4:8–9, 16–18; Galatians 6:9; Philippians 1:6; 4:6–7, 19; 1 Thessalonians 3:3; Hebrews 10:35–36; 1 Peter 1:6–9

Distraught/Upset:
Psalm 31:24; 61:1–2; 103:13–14; Luke 18:1–8; Hebrews 12:3; 13:5; 1 Peter 5:7

Doubting:
John 6:37; 10:27–29; Philippians 1:6; 2 Timothy 1:12; Hebrews 11:6; 12:2; 1 John 5:13

Far from God:
Psalm 139:1–18; Proverbs 28:13; Isaiah 55:7; Lamentations 3:22–23; Luke 15:11–24; Revelation 2:4–5

Jealous/Envious:
Exodus 20:17; Proverbs 14:30; 27:4; 1 Corinthians 3:3; Galatians 5:19–21, 26; Hebrews 13:5; James 3:16; 5:9

Lonely:
Psalm 25:16–18; Isaiah 46:4; 55:12; John 14:15–21; Acts 2:25–26; Hebrews 13:5–6

Mourning:
Psalm 23; Isaiah 25:8; John 11:25; 14:1–3; 1 Corinthians 15:55; 2 Corinthians 5:1; Philippians 1:21; 1 Thessalonians 4:13–18; 1 Peter 1:3–4

Sad:
Psalm 91:14–15; 119:50; Isaiah 43:2; 61:1–3; 2 Corinthians 1:3–4; 2 Thessalonians 2:16–17; Hebrews 4:15–16

Sick:
Exodus 15:26; 23:25; Psalm 30:2; 41:3; 91:3–10; 103:3–5; 107:20; Jeremiah 30:17; 33:6; Matthew 9:35; James 5:14–15; 3 John 2

Tempted:

Psalm 119:9–11; Matthew 4:1–4, 11; 1 Corinthians 10:12–13; James 1:2–3, 12–15; 4:7

Troubled by Wrong Thoughts:

Joshua 1:8; Psalm 1:1–6; 4:4; 19:7–14; Isaiah 26:3; Philippians 4:8; Colossians 3:2

ACKNOWLEDGMENTS

My ongoing journey in developing unshakable faith started in 1989 when I decided to become a Christian. But before that time and since, many have impacted the development of my spiritual foundation. They include but aren't limited to Alton and Patsy Searcy, Lela Butler, Bill and Sue Butler, Polly Branch, Ann Cannon, Doug Haulk, Bobby Gantt, David Jones, Boyce Gregory, Milton Hollifield and Rick Warren. In addition, my lifelong friends and colleagues have stood beside me and helped me stand strong when things have gone wrong.

I must also thank the members of The Journey Church teaching team, who provided invaluable insights into almost every chapter in this book. I must particularly highlight the immense contributions of my long-time colleagues, Pastors Kerrick Thomas and Jason Hatley.

I must also express a huge thanks to the members of The Journey Church—in all her locations—for your ongoing support and prayers. The teachings in the book were first written in community with you and first presented live before you. I love doing church with you!

My sincere appreciation goes out to the team at Faith Journey Books, which has made this book and many other similar resources possible. I must especially highlight the contributions of Sandra Olivieri and Raelyn Garriga. You have no idea the impact you are having on people around the world.

Jennifer Dykes Henson has been a partner and co-creator on over a dozen books, and to my ongoing amazement, she continues to reach new levels with each book. Her writing, editing and interpreting skills are hard to overstate. I cannot say thank you enough! Jennifer and her husband, Brian, serve as models of everything I discuss in this book.

Finally, I want to thank the love of my life, Kelley, and my son, Alexander. Kelley, I love you now more than ever! Thank you both for your dedication to this book and your unwavering support.

NOTES

1 Lewis, C. S. *Mere Christianity*. London: The MacMillan Company, 1952. p. 40-41.

2. Eyre, Stephen. "C. S. Lewis on Heaven and Hell." https://www.cslewisinstitute.org/resources/c-s-lewis-on-heaven-and-hell.

3. Merton, Thomas. *Thoughts in Solitude.* New York: Farrar, Straus & Cudahy, 1958. p. 79.

4. Maxwell, John C. *Failing Forward.* Nashville: Thomas Nelson, 2000. p. 3.

5. A Puritan's Mind, "John Owen: The Temptation of Believers." Accessed April 2, 2025. https://www.apuritansmind.com/puritan-favorites/john-owen/the-temptation-of-believers.

6. Bonhoeffer, Dietrich. *Creation and Fall: Temptation; Two Biblical Studies.* New York: Simon & Schuster, 1997, p. 51.

7. Collins, James C. *Good to Great: Why Some Companies Make the Leap - and Others Don't.* New York: HarperBusiness, 2001, p. 1.

8. Much of the outline for this chapter and some key teachings must be credited to the influence of Rick and Kay Warren, the founders of Saddleback Church in Southern California. I was on pastoral staff with them for several years as we prepared for parenthood. Rick and Kay provided many valuable lessons through their personal advice, seminars, and sermons. In fact, so much of what they taught me has been internalized over my years of child-rearing that it's challenging to differentiate between my own unique

thoughts and their teachings. I want to give credit where credit is due. The keys I outline below are written by me, but they are not only derived from scripture; they are also strongly adapted from the lessons, key phrases, and biblical insights I learned from Pastor Rick and his wife, Kay, who were wonderful examples of Unshakable parents.

9. Once again, I must thank Pastor Rick Warren for the phrasing of these four elements. Source: private conversations and various sermons during my time on staff at Saddleback Church.

10. King, Stephen. "Vassar Commencement Speech." StephenKing.com. May 20, 2001. https://stephenking.com/news/vassar-commencement-speech-107.html.

11. Sims, Margie. "Strategic Sex." *Today's Christian Woman.* www.todayschristianwoman.com/articles/2008/september/strategicsex.html.

12. "Staying Together Through Infidelity." iMom. 2010. http://www.imom.com/staying-together-through-infidelity.

13. Tozer, A. W., and James L. Snyder. *The Purpose of Man: Designed to Worship.* Ventura, CA: Regal, 2009. p. 107.

14. Giglio, Louie. *The Air I Breathe: Worship as a Way of Life.* Sisters, OR: Multnomah, 2003. p. 54.

15. Kübler-Ross, Elisabeth. *On Death and Dying.* New York: Scribner, 1969.

ABOUT NELSON SEARCY

Dr. Nelson Searcy is the Founding and Lead Pastor of The Journey Church, with locations across New York City and in Boca Raton, Florida. He and his wife, Kelley, have one son, Alexander. Nelson is a cancer survivor and the author of over 20 books, including *Breakthrough: Discovering God's Power for Your Problems*, the Revised and Updated edition of *The Greatness Principle: Finding Significance and Joy by Serving Others*, and *The Generosity Ladder: Your Next Step to Financial Peace*. See www.NelsonSearcyBooks.com for more. After becoming a Christian in college, Nelson entered full-time ministry in 1990. He has served with Rick Warren at Saddleback Church in Southern California. Today Nelson and The Journey Church appear routinely on lists such as "The 50 Most Influential Churches" and "The 25 Most Innovative Leaders." As founder of ChurchLeaderInsights.com, he's trained more than 50,000 church leaders, with over 3,500 of them being church planters. Nelson holds a BA and BS from Gardner Webb University, MDiv from Duke University and DLitt from Louisiana Baptist University. His continued mission is to help church leaders and church members around the world cooperate with God to fulfill the Great Commission.

A PERSONAL NOTE FROM THE AUTHOR

As a cancer survivor, transplant recipient and overachiever when it comes to having major surgeries, I invite you to consider these steps:

1) Regular blood donation.
Visit this website: **RedCross.org/give-blood**

2) Organ donation. You can potentially help up to seven people and I know it's a prayerful decision. Learn more at **OrganDonor.gov**

3) Getting screened as early and as often as you can for all kinds of cancer.
Develop a regular plan with your family doctor and dermatologist. Almost 40% of Americans will be diagnosed with cancer during their lifetimes.

Honor God with your body,

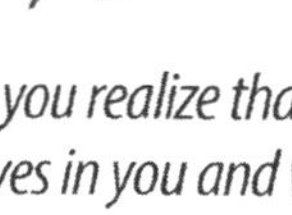

"Don't you realize that your body is the temple of the Holy Spirit, who lives in you and was given to you by God? You do not belong to yourself, for God bought you with a high price. So you must honor God with your body." — 1 Corinthians 6:19-20 (NLT)